Getting Back to Work

How to Piece Your Well-Being Back Together When Unemployment Strikes at Midlife

Kelly A. Clark, PhD

How to Piece Your Well-Being Back Together When Unemployment Strikes at Midlife © 2024 Kelly A. Clark, PhD

Published by Winter Island Press, Salem, MA.
Winterislandpress.com

ISBN: 979-8-9878655-2-1

Editing and design assistance by Holbrook Author Services

WINTER ISLAND PRESS

Dedication

In honor of the people who openly shared their experiences, stories, learnings, struggles and insights in hopes that their unemployment voyage would help others.

Table of Contents

The People You Will Meet on Their Journey Through Unemployment...

Introduction i

1. Safeguarding Your Wellness: The Pieces of the Well-Being Framework 1

    The Well-Being Framework 4

    Behavioral Coping Strategies............................... 6

    Cognitive Maneuvers   7

2. Stick to a Daily Routine 9

    Act Now! 16

    Resources.. 17

3. The Hunt for Work 18

    Structuring Your Job Search............................... 20

    Access Employment Counseling   21

    Fend Off Age Discrimination.............................. 22

    Seeking Work.. 25

    Pursue Training and Education........................... 27

    Act Now! 30

4. Slash Your Budget 31

    Identify Needs Versus Wants 33

    Adjust Your Budget 34

Renegotiate and Restructure Debt 35

Seek Financial Assistance 36

Work Part-time 36

Reassess Living Arrangements.......................... 37

Try Bartering and Time Banking 39

Assess Your Timeline 41

Act Now! 42

5. Balance Your Job Search with Meaningful Activities 43

Balancing Job Search with Other Productive Activities   45

Act Now! 52

6. Access Social Support 55

General Support.............................. 57

Emotional Support 58

Encouragement.............................. 59

The Value of Networking 60

How to Improve Your Social Network 61

Act Now! 63

Resources 63

7. Build Mental Strength 64

Self-Awareness 67

Optimism.............................. 69

Cognitive Reappraisal.............................. 71

Reframing Negative Events 72

Reframing Work Identity. 73

Reframing View of Self.............................. 74

How to Shift Perspective and Reframe Situations 74

Using Positive Mantra.. 76

Mantras for Job Seekers 77

Act Now! 78

Additional Reading... 79

8. Take Charge 80

Personal Agency... 83

Six-Step Model to Catalyze Change 84

Be a Learner 85

Determination.. 86

Don't Blame Yourself 87

Avoid Social Media Self-Sabotage 88

Enhance Your Agency   88

Act Now! 90

Further Reading   90

9. Piecing Your Well-Being Back Together 91

Engage in Meaningful Activities 92

Maintain a Structured Schedule 95

Conserve Resources... 96

Access Social Support 98

Build Mental Strength.. 99

The Well-Being Framework 100

Closing   101

10. Where Are They Now? 103

Uprooted & Resettled Elena.. 103

Re-employed & Retired Walter 108

Homeless & Resettled Lou 114

Staying the Course Pablo 120

Deferred Retirement Tzippora... 125

11. Don't Sit Idle **132**

Acknowledgements **134**

About the Author **135**

Endnotes **136**

The People You Will Meet on Their Journey Through Unemployment

This book features real people at midlife who, in adversity, figured out how to cope and maintain their well-being while proactively searching for work. They employed specific strategies to bounce back from job loss, find their way in a new reality, and stay open to new opportunities. Here is a brief description of each of the 15 people who shared their experience.

Anna

Anna, age 58, previously worked from home as an aluminum framing estimator. Two weeks after she was laid off, she was diagnosed with a severe case of Lyme disease, which impacted her physical and cognitive abilities. Anna had been unemployed for over 14 months. She was married and held a bachelor's degree. She exhausted her retirement accounts and cashed everything out to pay for medical expenses.

Aaron

Aaron, age 49, previously worked as a digital mapping technician for a Belgian company that was purchased by another Belgian company. Aaron had been unemployed for 26 months, was single and held a bachelor's degree.

Elena

Elena, age 49, previously worked in the staffing industry, as director of sales and marketing. She reported that she increased sales over her five-year tenure by 183% and was one of the highest paid employees. Elena had been unemployed for

30 months. She was married and held a bachelor's degree. Her unemployment had expired, and she was on the verge of tapping into her retirement funds.

Helen

Helen, age 53, previously worked as a laboratory technician for an environmental science company. The company reduced its workforce and was utilizing temporary employees for technician work. Helen had been unemployed for 17 months, was married, and held a bachelor's degree.

John

John, age 53, recently obtained his associate degree and graduated with high honors. He was a union industrial electrician, a certified nuclear electrician, and possessed security clearances for the nuclear industry in the U.S. He had worked in this field for over 30 years. John's wife was a cancer patient.

Kate

Kate, age 57, previously worked as a customer service representative for a retail business for approximately five years. There was a reorganization of the business and as a result Kate was laid off. She had been unemployed for nine months. Kate was divorced and had an associate degree.

Lance

Lance, age 47, was married and had four children between the ages of 9 and 15. Lance held a bachelor's degree and was employed for 25 years in the financial services industry. He held his last position for 10 years. Lance had been unemployed for 16 months.

Lou

Lou, age 51, held a bachelor's degree. His wife worked during the school year in a middle-school cafeteria. Lou previously worked in the computer and information technology support field. He held his last position for eight years. Lou had been unemployed for over three years.

Pablo

Pablo, age 52, worked as a technician at a television station for 26 years, until he was laid off. After two months of unemployment, Pablo obtained a part-time job doing similar work at a different television station. He was considered a freelance employee and covered shifts as needed. He did not have any set hours or days and worked on average 20 hours a week. He was single and held a bachelor's degree.

Remy

Remy, age 55, was married and had a high school diploma. Remy previously worked at a family-owned woman's shop as a sales associate and beauty advisor. The shop closed, leaving Remy unemployed for over 10 months.

Rob

Rob, age 53, previously worked for 23 years as a printing press operator. He was laid off from this position and had been unemployed for about nine months. He was married and held a high school diploma.

Terry

Terry, age 50, held a high school diploma. Terry's husband worked full-time. Terry worked most of her life in the accounting field. She was initially laid off from her accounting job and was subsequently reemployed as an assembly worker at a manufacturing company for about two years. She had been unemployed for two years and her unemployment compensation had expired.

Tom

Tom, age 57, had one year of college completed. He had been unemployed for 15 months. Tom had worked in the cable industry. He was with his prior employer for 24 years. Tom was married.

Tzippora

Tzippora, age 57, was divorced and had a daughter in college. She was a technical writer and held a bachelor's and master's degree in geology. She most recently worked from her home office as a contractor for a computer company and she was employed for about a year and a half before becoming unemployed. During this same period, Tzippora found out she had breast cancer. She finished her radiation treatments the day after she was laid off. She had been unemployed for over seven months.

Walter

Walter, age 57, was married and had attended three years of college. Walter was a veteran and noted having been in more stressful circumstances than the loss of a job. He previously worked as a telecommunications technician, selling, installing, maintaining, and servicing analog telephone systems. He had been unemployed for a little over eight months. Walter also reported having Attention Deficit Hyperactivity Disorder (ADHD).

Introduction

Midway through the journey of our life, I found myself within a forest dark, for the straightforward pathway had been lost.
     – Dante's *Inferno*

For eight years, Anna had worked as an estimator for an aluminum framing company until the day she received an out-of-the-blue phone call from her supervisor. Her position had been eliminated.

"I was extremely upset," Anna said. "I was the breadwinner for my family. I had no idea what I was going to do. I was losing the bulk of my income." Anna, at age 58, suddenly found herself unemployed at midlife. She had become a victim of the 2008 recession.

Over the years, Anna had been steadily employed in the construction field. She worked as an estimator for a variety of construction companies and had managed a team of estimators throughout her career. "I felt useless, discarded, like I was damaged or something," Anna said. "I was angry and at the same time thinking, 'Well nobody told me they had any issues regarding my work being wrong or inadequate.' No one had said anything."

At about the same time, Anna had started to notice changes in the way she felt every day. She was tired, she experienced certain cognitive issues and some challenges speaking. "It turned out two weeks after I was laid off, I was diagnosed with Lyme disease," Anna said. "The disease was in my joints and had entered my brain. Along with losing my job, I lost my health insurance. I didn't know how I was going to pay for my medical expenses. I couldn't apply for jobs given my physical and cognitive challenges."

The first six months were horrific for Anna. She felt damaged, physically, and mentally, with nowhere to turn. "My confidence level dropped so far that I had a couple of days where I was suicidal. I felt so worthless," Anna said. "It was hard on the family. I was sick, lying in bed, taking these shots that cost a fortune and I couldn't go to work. We had lost more than 50 percent of our income."

It was months before Anna felt well enough to apply for unemployment insurance. "I mean, what was I going to do? Go in there and go, yeah, I can go to work? Are you kidding me? I had no idea if I could work. I couldn't go for an interview, even. So, I waited almost six months before I filed a claim. At that point, I could manage with the antibiotics I was prescribed."

A restlessness stirred within Anna as she came out of the dense fog of her illness. "I woke up one day, and went, okay, I still felt like a broken person, but I was well, and my health was better. I've always talked about wanting to volunteer, so I started volunteering as a cook one Saturday at a homeless shelter and ended up doing it three times a month. I found that I thoroughly enjoyed it, and that volunteering helped me." With each passing day, the tension built. "It's stressful on the marriage and everything because you have to watch the money," Anna said. "I would question if it was okay to buy new underwear, really. It sounds ridiculous but that's how penny-pinched we were. We cut expenses wherever we could cut them, anything, and everything we could possibly do. I mean I had no fear of saying, 'I don't have a job. Can you give me a better price?' And really, anything, we just did what we could and cut back."

Anna's 27-year-old son moved back in with her and her husband to help offset expenditures. They had a one-bedroom condo. Everyone sacrificed privacy and adjusted schedules to make it work. "I don't really have any money left," Anna said. "I have no retirement accounts left. I had to cash everything out. So, I don't have anything. Our savings went to pay for the medical expenses for me."

Countless people, like Anna, experience pain and face obstacles as they struggle with job loss. You may be one of them. But you are clearly not alone.

The loss of a job brings with it all the intensity and hurt that you experience in other monumental life loss. When you lose your job, you are expected to immediately turn the page and begin the search for a new job, which requires being confident, proactive, and outward-focused at a time when you simply want to hunker down and isolate from the world. Anna was one of these people.

My interest in the topic of coping with the adversity of job loss evolved out of my three decades of working as a nonprofit executive. Over the years I have served in a variety of positions, including the Regional Vice President for AARP, Chief Operating Officer for NH Public Broadcasting, and President of the Workforce Opportunity Council. During this time, I have worked with a variety of people as they made employment transitions, both voluntary and involuntary. These experiences shaped and contributed to my curiosity about why some people get through job loss more easily than others. This, coupled with the fact that the experiences of older unemployed people are understudied, fueled my interest and ultimately became the focus of my dissertation.

In 2011, I spent six months crisscrossing New Hampshire to hear the life stories of people who had been through wrenching changes and still reported positive well-being on the General

Health Questionnaire (GHQ-12). Anna was one of the individuals I met.

So, how *do* you maintain your well-being after the loss of a job at midlife? That is the question which this book sets out to answer through the eyes of 15 long-term unemployed people from New Hampshire. These people had careers and worked in white-collar and blue-collar occupations. They were retail workers; technicians working in telecommunications, television, digital mapping, the environmental sciences; information technology workers; industrial and nuclear engineers; sales and marketing, financial services, and technical writing professionals.

Little did I know how very relevant my discoveries would become during the challenging time of the COVID-19 pandemic. As a result of the pandemic, over 20 million Americans lost their jobs between March and April 2020. The economy tumbled recklessly out of control, and at its highest point, unemployment was at a Great Depression-level of 14.7%.

While unemployment rates have decreased since 2021, this trend was not experienced homogeneously across all populations. Average durations of unemployment for older workers are longer than durations experienced by younger age groups, especially during economic downturns. The percentage of jobseekers ages 55 and over who were long-term unemployed in March of 2024 was 24 percent as compared to 19.9 percent for job seekers age 16 to 54.[1] Even during the historically tight labor market which existed in 2022, there were some 1.1 million individuals in the United States who were long-term unemployed, or out of work.

The frequency with which workers face job loss and the duration of unemployment for people at mid-life underscores the importance of understanding how people safeguard their well-being during a time of traumatic loss and isolation. This book is about Anna and people like her. It is about the practical steps and actions some people took to stay positive and proactive under the dire circumstances of being unemployed and the strain of searching for a new job.

Readers will learn what practical tips and approaches helped these individuals maintain a positive outlook while undergoing dire emotional and financial stress. These tips and approaches are organized into the Well-Being Framework which highlights five overarching strategies for staying afloat and optimizing your prospects for rejoining the workforce. Readers will learn how to create a personalized plan based upon these successful strategies.

This is a book, therefore, for anyone who has received the sort of phone call that Anna did. It is also for loved ones, friends, and colleagues struggling to understand and help. The people you will meet tell impassioned stories of coping, adapting, remaining optimistic, and wresting value out of a very challenging circumstance. I invite you to join me as I share their inspiration and hope and as I illuminate how they effectively put the well-being pieces back together to rebuild their life and to sustain that hope.

And so the journey starts.

1. Safeguarding Your Wellness: The Pieces of the Well-Being Framework

It was a Tuesday in early October. I was to meet Tom at the One-Stop employment services office at noon. As I drove into the parking lot, the United States flag fluttered high above on a white flagpole that fronted the building. The leaves from the maple trees adjacent to the building had begun to fall and carpet the recently mowed grass that surrounded the building.

The office was abuzz with people working at a bank of computers and with others waiting for meetings with employment counselors. I was greeted by the receptionist, and then was escorted back to a small conference room.

Tom arrived promptly. He was in his early fifties, of medium height, and round-shouldered. His eyes were close-set and a deep hazel. He looked much younger than his age. He greeted me in a husky voice, and said, "I just came from one of those job networking meetings, so I'm kind of in a little up mode today. I find those meetings kind of enlightening." Tom pulled a chair out and took a seat across from me at the conference table.

Tom had been with the same employer for 24 years. He had started out as a cable installer and worked his way up in the company to become a senior telecom manager. At the time he was laid off, he had been leading an applications software team focused on data collection and management. He spoke with pride about his work and the engineers and developers he had supervised. "My team was supportive," Tom said. "When it became clear that a layoff was imminent, the team proposed taking on a challenging project and completing it so that I could list it as one of my accomplishments." In the end, Tom was a victim of a national-level reorganization.

When I spoke with Tom, he had been unemployed for 15 months and had four months of unemployment benefits remaining. He indicated that the pressures of unemployment were taking a toll on his marriage. "It has been putting an awful lot of stress on the relationship. I think the first year, my wife had been pretty good about it," Tom said. "And now she's kind of getting edgy and asking more frequently about my job prospects." Psychologically, unemployment can really take a toll. "You get a feeling of no self-worth. You must combat that on almost a daily basis."

As a child, Tom had moved around quite a bit, approximately 12 times in 10 years. "My father was in the service, so I was always in a different school, and I was the new kid," Tom said. "That has helped prepare me for this kind of thing. People say losing your job is like death. No, it's worse. It's like divorce because you still must see the people you worked with occasionally."

Tom had dropped out of high school in the seventh grade. He eventually completed his GED and followed in his father's footsteps, enrolling in the Army first, and then the Air Force. "I was infantry. So, my job was to shoot guns at people and do very bad things to them," Tom said. "When I went into the Air Force, I excelled at that. I ramped up to instructor in two years. I was an aero-medical evacuation instructor. I learned to kill people first and then I learned to put them back together." After 10 years of military service, Tom had found his way into the cable television industry, and he continued serving his country in the National Guard.

In some ways, though, the transition was a welcome change for Tom. "To an extent, the layoff was a great relief because I was aware of the corporate politics and they were not making business decisions," Tom said. "Corporate decisions were being driven by the politics of the board of directors, major shareholders, and favoritism." He asked if I watched *Survivor*, a reality competition television show.

I said, "No and why?"

Tom said, "When you watch *Survivor*, sometimes the strongest people get voted off the island early, and sometimes it is the weakest. You don't know which one you are. So that is what corporate life was like. It was like *Survivor*. You didn't know if you would have a job tomorrow or not. And everybody was backstabbing each other to get ahead." It was helpful that Tom was able to recognize aspects of his former job that had caused him tension and angst.

To stay on track and fight off the psychological toll, Tom got up every day at 6:30 a.m., as he did when he was working. This was an important practice. He explained that he would start doing things immediately and that he avoided the television for fear of becoming a lazy person. During the initial months of unemployment, he focused on his education and expanding his skill set, which was an excellent approach. In this way, he was using his time in meaningful ways, which helped. His hope was to make the transition from the cable industry to IT. He explored several IT industry certifications that would position him competitively in the job market. He became certified as a Cisco certified network associate (CCNA) and started to take online courses that would lead to a bachelor of science in information technologies.

In addition to advancing his education, Tom invested his time in other worthy causes. He volunteered in his local community and took on leadership positions. He helped to create the first energy commission for his local town and served as its chairman. He was also elected by the town to the budget committee and took on the role of vice-chairman. His work with both groups provided the opportunity to interact with people, to network, and to ward off the isolation that often results from being long-term unemployed. These were all positive and proactive steps that Tom took. As he reflected on the benefits of his volunteer work, he explained how his contributions helped him to realize that the layoff wasn't about him and his abilities: "Because when you get terminated, you do have that self-doubt, no matter how optimistic you are and no matter how skilled you are. So that's why I needed to do this volunteer work—to reassure myself that it wasn't me."

> *"Because when you get terminated, you do have that self-doubt, no matter how optimistic you are and no matter how skilled you are. So that's why I needed to do this volunteer work—to reassure myself that it wasn't me"*

The Well-Being Framework

I talked to several people like Tom. They all struggled to remain optimistic and proactive after months of rejection, social shunning, financial stress, and worry. Their individual stories and experiences revealed straightforward steps anyone can take to protect their well-being while carrying on with the search for work.

The Well-Being Framework emerged from my discussions with people experiencing long-term unemployment at mid-life. Collectively, they utilized a similar suite of coping strategies to cushion the negative impacts of job loss. Their stories shared several behavioral and cognitive coping strategies—accessing social support, maintaining a structured schedule, engaging in productive and meaningful activities, managing financial resources and having a positive mindset—that together buffered the trauma of job loss and enabled them to remain active in their job search, despite obstacles.

The Well-Being Framework

Another person I met, Heidi, applied several of the strategies noted in this framework. She previously had worked in the financial services industry, which was hit hard during the 2008 recession. She had been one of 800 people laid off from her company. Heidi was matter-of-fact about how she was managing.

"I've been through this before, I know I can survive it again. I just go about re-stacking the dominoes in my life. You know, live small, reassess expenses, cut back, have a conversation or several with my kids about new expectations, that kind of thing," Heidi said. "So, it was more about falling back on what I do best, which is project management. Project management of my life. What are the cards that I've been dealt? What are the things that I have control over? How can I mitigate the risk? Identify it – mitigate it – and plan. That's basically what I did."

While getting her personal life in order, Heidi also involved others. After a month, she reached out to eight or so of her laid-off colleagues with an idea to start a new organization. They met for dinner on a cold New Hampshire night in February to figure out how they would support each other to find work. Heidi talked about helping others, as well as setting the resentment or anger aside. Out of the conversation, a new organization, Network for Work, was born and quickly grew to a 900-person online community. The focus of the organization was to foster connections and help the unemployed establish networks for their career development. In addition, Heidi started to co-host a radio show to get the word out about Network for Work.

Heidi's story illuminates two distinct coping strategies that she and others have drawn on to help them survive long-term unemployment. One is how she thought about her problem (the cognitive dimension), and the other was what she did about it (the behavioral dimension). Let's take a quick look at the different strategies.

Behavioral Coping Strategies

Behavioral coping refers to the way someone acts or controls themselves. Behaviors are observable. People I spoke with utilized a range of behavioral approaches to cope. Some accessed social support networks to fight off isolation and loneliness. Many people proactively engaged in a variety of meaningful activities such as caregiving, volunteering, and hobbies. Others pursued training and education to bolster their range of marketable skills, which, in turn, made them more competitive in the search for work. Research has shown that an important determinant of well-being during unemployment is people's involvement in meaningful activities.

Tom joined the Society of Cable Television Engineers, or SCTE. He became a board member and took on planning the annual golf fundraiser. "The work on the annual golf event, monthly conference calls, and participating in SCTE have kept me in the ballpark professionally," Tom said. Tom's proactive steps to be involved helped keep his skills current and fought off isolation by engaging with others.

Cognitive Maneuvers

Cognitive coping strategies seek to manage the emotional response to stress, and the phrase refers to activities aimed at addressing the negative feelings and consequences of stressful events, like job loss. People can reframe their situation, apply personal agency, rely on self-confidence, and hold on to a sense of optimism.

Pablo, who previously worked as a technician at a local television station, was determined not to be broken. "I don't surrender myself to the situation I find myself in," Pablo said. "It's like the woman who was supposed to be helping me get training; she was not following through, so I made it happen myself." Pablo appropriately took charge to influence the outcome he was seeking.

Many others similarly expressed an intention to stay positive and to put the experience of job loss into perspective, which is a solid strategy. "I mean, when I start doing the little pity party I just look around and say okay, you could have this or that, or you've got X number of days to live, you know," Tom said. "I've known people that have been in that situation. So, it isn't as bad as you think."

While it is easy to say that you should be optimistic and proactive like Tom and Pablo, the truth is, after you have been out of work for several months, it's not easy to maintain these outlooks and activities. However, there are actionable steps that can be taken and applied by anyone in this situation.

In the chapters to come, people share heart-wrenching

stories about difficult and adverse situations, and inspiring stories about how these situations were overcome. Taken together, the stories offer lessons that reinforce the pieces of the Well-Being Framework, which offers a path out of the unemployment wilderness.

2. Stick to a Daily Routine

Maintain A Structured Schedule

A glimpse of the Ammonoosuc River came into view as I turned into the parking lot of the unemployment office. A deep green grass border surrounded the building and added warmth to the otherwise cold metal structure. From the outside, I might have surmised that I was visiting an automotive body shop or a manufacturing facility. The metal structure formerly owned by Littleton Coin Company is now home to the Littleton Learning Center, a one-stop center for career and educational services.

Walter arrived promptly at noon. He greeted me with a cordial and yet commanding voice. He took in every detail of the room with precision through his sharp chestnut-brown eyes. He wore a crewcut, was fair-skinned, and stood about five foot eight inches in height. He was a barrel-chested man who looked like he exercised regularly. His presence suggested qualities of pride, honor, and integrity.

He listened intently as I inquired about his experience with unemployment. Walter explained that he was in his late 50s, married, and had completed three years of college. He and his wife, Cara, chose not to have children, though they had several nieces and nephews they helped financially. They also kept a watchful eye on Walter's divorced parents, who were in their 80s. Walter described himself as a fervent capitalist and a Libertarian. He had served in the Army military police for four years. His primary assignment there was to protect lives and property on Army installations by enforcing military laws and regulations, as well as controlling traffic, preventing crime, and responding to emergencies. He had trained at Fort Leonard Wood, Missouri. While he did not see direct combat, Walter said, "As a veteran, I have experienced more stressful circumstances than job loss, and perhaps I am more resilient as a result."

He talked with pride about his employer and his tenure. He had previously worked as a telecommunications technician. Walter sold, installed, maintained, and serviced analog telephone systems. "My résumé is a mile and a half deep and two inches wide as far as specialization goes," Walter said. He had received rave customer reviews, and a few corporate-wide improvements he had suggested had been adopted.

At the time I spoke with Walter, he had been unemployed for a little over eight months. A few months before he was laid off, Walter had booked a mountain lion hunt in Arizona. He loved to hike, hunt, and shoot firearms. He had been holding off on booking the trip, and then the president of the company, which was headquartered in Texas, made a visit to the Boston branch for an all-hands meeting. "At the meeting the president confirmed what we'd seen in e-mails about the company being sold," Walter said. "The president was upbeat and reassured us that now there would be terrific opportunities for everyone in the room, and the future of the company was bright. I went home and made a non-refundable deposit on the trip, booked the hotel and the flight." Ten days later the company laid off 35 people nationwide, and Walter was one of those individuals.

Walter did not feel crushed by the layoff. He did not take the layoff personally, which helped him keep things in perspective. "I knew it was not due to a lack of performance, a bad relationship with my employer, or any of those things," Walter said. He attributed the loss of employment to the downturn in the market, a shift in technology and the economy. "I had somewhat anticipated it and prepared as best I could."

Walter continued to start each day by reading two papers,

the *New Hampshire Union Leader,* and the *Boston Globe.* "I'm a political junkie and a news junkie," Walter said. "I'll go through some political blogs once a day just to see if there's a story that I read in the morning newspaper that offers a different angle." Walter added, "I am getting up at 5:30 in the morning. I'm doing that now because I did it before, when I was working, and I think I'm going to need to do it again, no matter where I'm working. It will be a fixed, rigid schedule, and if I don't keep it in between jobs, I lose my level of civilization."

Walter underscores two very important practices. First, he maintains a schedule. Routines and schedules provide a reassuring structure to daily life. A schedule helps us feel in control, provides some certainty and predictability. The second critical point Walter conveys is the importance of a daily sleep schedule. He does not fall prey to the gravitational pull of his bed or the television. He rises and goes to bed at a consistent time. This helps the body feel less fatigued and contributes to physical and mental well-being.

The structure created by a daily work routine serves as the scaffolding for our life.

When a job is lost the scaffolding falters. The maintenance of a structured schedule with meaningful activity helps to preserve a sense of identity, competence, and self-esteem.

Begin each day by getting up at roughly the same time you would if you were working. Set your alarm clock for the same time each weekday. And keep a standard bedtime too. Consistently maintain these hours on typical workdays.

Introduce small acts of structure into your day, like scheduling breaks and a time for lunch and time to wind down at the end of the day.

Walter described using a diagram in his mind to plan his day, just like when he was working. "So, sort of mentally setting up a decision tree or a flowchart in my mind of what was going to happen today, without carving it in stone. And I still do that now. I make a list of the things I must do. As I sit for breakfast, I turn the TV off and I go over my list. I mentally say okay, today I have a meeting at 1:00, I must do this, I must do that, I must update my LinkedIn profile, etc."

While it may be tempting to sleep in and spend the day doing what you'd like, and then looking for work when the spirit strikes, avoid this temptation at all costs. Just as having a schedule will help you to feel productive and optimistic, not having a schedule will lead you to procrastinate, and in time you'll feel bored, lazy, and your self-esteem will plummet. Schedule two days a week as your "days off" and do whatever you want. But five days a week, get up, suit up, and show up. You're far more likely to remain optimistic and find work if you do so.

I found that it was not unusual for resilient people to be intentional and to create rules for themselves. Elena had been the director of sales and marketing for a staffing company and had been unemployed for 30 months. "I have some rules, some unemployment rules for myself," Elena said. "One is I never watched TV, not one time during the day ever. I'm always busy. I always have things to do. And that's what I focus on. I never sit around. Even when I don't have tasks, I make tasks. So, I stay engaged one way or another."

Write down your schedule and keep a print or electronic version in front of you to review daily. Be creative, make it your own, explore free calendar tools online.

> *The point is to develop a schedule that will work for you. Map out a schedule for when you will work on your job search, exercise, take care of household chores, work on a hobby, refine a talent or skill, and wind down for the day.*

Filling your schedule with meaningful activities will also help take away some of the frustration and stress associated with seeking out a new job and the rejection that naturally occurs. Let's look at how Walter filled his days.

Walter had enrolled in training to obtain specialized certifications in digital networks and converged networks (telephone and internet). "I have recently been diagnosed with ADHD and I need in-person, face-to-face training," Walter said. He had used his time wisely and updated his skills and learned the digital side of the industry, which provided a know-how transferable to modern phone systems and computer networks. Walter appeared confident about finding a job. "It is a matter of when, and not if, I find a job. I'm in a lifeboat, but I can see the shore and the wind is blowing that way. So, it's not like I'm a Pollyanna, but realistically, I'll find something."

Throughout the ups and downs of unemployment, Walter did not lose sight of the importance of his interests and hobbies, and the need to balance his time with activities unrelated to his search for work. He took several courses at Sig Sauer Academy in Epping, where firearms skills can be enhanced. "It is great training with military, former military people, active duty, police, FBI, sky marshals and EMTs,"

Walter said. "I have an interest in the field, but realistically I do not have the credentials to make that kind of a career transition." Walter also went on the lion hunt that he had booked and paid for just before he had been laid off. He met some people with whom he continued to stay in contact, which he found helpful in combating the loss of social connection with his former work colleagues.

Another of Walter's hobbies was singing. Every Friday night Walter and Cara would go to Sullivans Irish Pub, a little place in the next town, where they would join a small group of traditional Irish-style musicians. One played the guitar and banjo, one played tin whistle and drum, one played fiddle and guitar, and Walter sang. He described how important his time singing was to him. "Singing brings respite, I am with interesting people, and it's fun to do. And that is good, again for morale, and it's part of the structure."

Others leveraged their time to develop a hobby or personal interest or skill. Rob had an ability to train dogs and worked this into his regular schedule as part of his typical day during unemployment. "I also have been involved with other people's dogs. I have a knack for this, and I've cultivated it over the years. And I work with problem dogs," Rob said. "So right now, I have a dog living with me that's with the German Shorthaired Pointer Rescue Association of New England. And I'm doing some rehabilitation with her. So, I bring her to busy places. I'm juggling part-time jobs. Staying active and fit. I am helping friends and neighbors and enjoying the company of the dogs."

Rob was able to supplement his income while doing something he enjoyed and found rewarding. By taking an inventory of your skills and talents, you might just be able to commodify them while you are looking for work.

It is important to build in time for activities that feed your soul, as Walter and Rob did. Schedule time to exercise or read or work on a hobby or simply reach out to a friend or relative.

Make yourself accountable to yourself and others. Find a buddy or someone you can review your weekly schedule with and commit to it. Set manageable goals for time each day you would like to spend on each activity and see if you can hit each goal each workday. Start small and increase the time increments as your routine takes shape.

Establish a schedule for yourself, preferably one that mimics the schedule you kept when you were employed. Wake up every morning at a set time, get dressed, and be at your desk looking for work at the same time each day. Schedule breaks and days off, just as you would if you were employed. The more you can maintain a schedule, the more you will feel as if you are making progress, even when no job offers are coming in. By having a structure to your day, you will be less inclined to feel depressed, more apt to feel hopeful and optimistic, and more likely to eventually secure a job.

Take the time to build in shut-down rituals or routines that signal the end of the day. You might take a walk, transition to cook dinner, practice an instrument, or simply do the laundry. What you do doesn't matter, just do something to replace the routine of leaving the office and commuting home.

Lastly, since you are now working from home full-time, the tendency will be for the lines to blur between your search for work and your home life. Your professional and personal life will no longer be demarcated by the moment you walk through the front door of your home, but instead by the kitchen table or room you now conduct your job search from. Dividing your time between personal and professional is critical. If you are not careful, they will bleed together, which will contribute to burnout, and your job search will suffer.

Act Now!

- ✓ Plan your day and week.
- ✓ Write down your schedule and keep a print or electronic version in front of you to review daily. Be creative, make it your own, and explore free calendar tools online.
- ✓ Determine the hours you will focus on your job search daily and commit to this schedule.
- ✓ Complement the time searching for work with activities that feed your soul.
- ✓ Explore hobbies and areas of interest that might bring in some income.
- ✓ Build in "shut-down" rituals to end your day.

Resources

A weekly planner can help schedule your days and time to look for work as well as for activites.

Go to www.kellyclarkauthor.com for a sample.

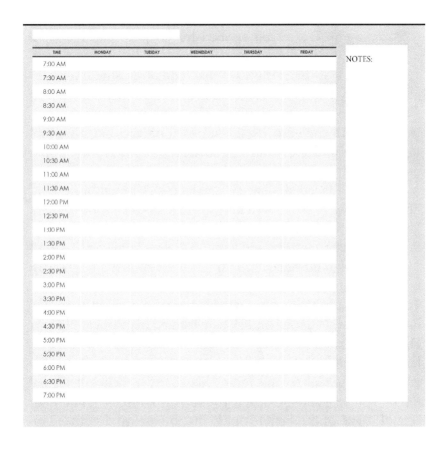

TIME	MONDAY	TUESDAY	WEDNESDAY	THURSDAY	FRIDAY	NOTES:
7:00 AM						
7:30 AM						
8:00 AM						
8:30 AM						
9:00 AM						
9:30 AM						
10:00 AM						
10:30 AM						
11:00 AM						
11:30 AM						
12:00 PM						
12:30 PM						
1:00 PM						
1:30 PM						
2:00 PM						
2:30 PM						
3:00 PM						
3:30 PM						
4:00 PM						
4:30 PM						
5:00 PM						
5:30 PM						
6:00 PM						
6:30 PM						
7:00 PM						

3. The Hunt for Work

Maintain A Structured Schedule

No matter how strictly you keep to a schedule, if you are unemployed, you have probably been hunting for work for ages, and are ready to give up. Have you applied for 50 jobs, and received ten rejections and 40 didn't even reply? Have you had one promising interview after another, yet none has resulted in a job offer? The truth is that looking for work is a full-time job itself, and as time goes on, that job becomes less and less rewarding as the rejections pile up. Don't despair.

Lance had faced similar circumstances. Through his story, he shares how he structured his time to focus on his job search, leveraged free employment counseling, persisted even with a flood of rejection letters, and kept up to date in his profession.

Lance was a bit out of breath   as he smiled and greeted me. He was trim and athletic-looking and sported an emerald Titleist golf shirt that accentuated his jewel-like green eyes. His hair was neatly clipped and closely framed his elongated face. He quickly explained that he thought he might be a few minutes late as he had to drop his children off to school. Then his youngest son realized he forgot his soccer practice gear, so Lance had to make a second round-trip between home and school. "One of the benefits of being unemployed is that I'm more accessible to help out with the children," Lance said. "I am also able to assist with caregiving for our parents. My wife's mother had a stroke in February and my mother had a bout of cancer last year."

Lance, age 47, had four dependent children between the

ages of nine and 15. He held a bachelor's degree, and had been employed for 25 years in the financial services industry. He had spent the first 20 years of his career as a project manager in the technology and business operations space. "So, I have tons of project management experience," Lance said. "But I don't have any formal certification." Lance had been promoted five years ago and was serving in the role of vice president for finance and development at the time of his termination. He had been unemployed for 16 months when I spoke with him.

Lance was a victim of a reduction in force. He had been aware that he could be laid off, but it was still a shock. "When it actually happens to you it is a little different," Lance said. "I think probably everybody thinks, at some level, they're indispensable in their role. I was initially shocked and surprised and resentful."

Lance had been working steadily since he graduated from college. He had been fortunate to have a bit of a financial cushion and severance resources, so he decided to take a few months off to enjoy time with his family. He started searching for work more aggressively at the end of the summer, but then landed in the hospital with a severe case of appendicitis and a variety of complications. The hospitalization had been a wake-up call. "So, from a quality-of-life standpoint, the emergency hospitalization triggered doctor follow-ups, the need to lose weight, get more exercise, and eat better," Lance said. "Over the past year, I went to a dietician, got more exercise, and my health and quality of life improved."

Lance enjoyed being home and having the extra time with his children. "The part that is gnawing away at me is I've got to get a job, and what happens if I don't get a job," he said. "So, I have to kind of come up with a plan. The financial aspect is bothersome. I'd just like to find employment sooner than later."

Seeking out a new job or new career became job number one

for Lance. "I'd say I spend about 30-35 hours per week searching for work," he said. "I dedicated five hours a day, five to seven days a week to my job search." Lance and people like him utilized their time to access free employment counseling, attend networking groups, conduct job searches, fine-tune their résumés, update their LinkedIn profiles, customize cover letters, and seek out additional training and education.

The job search and related efforts filled a substantial portion of Lance's daily schedule. Having a plan, as he did, for your job search and for how you spend your time in general is critical.

Structuring Your Job Search

A few tips surfaced from the people I spoke with about how to structure the time spent searching for work. They include the following:

- Determine which part of your day to focus on the job search and for how long.
- Schedule your time as you would a work schedule.
- Set a goal to spend a certain amount of time on your job search daily, and then use a timer to ensure that you do so.
- Test your schedule and try to ensure that your job search activities occur during the time of day when you have your greatest energy and focus.
- Be flexible and do not over-schedule your job search.
- Track progress and celebrate your daily efforts.

Access Employment Counseling

Most of the people I spoke with engaged in free employment counseling available through the One-Stop Job Centers. The Job Centers are in every state and provide a full range of free assistance to job seekers under one roof. The centers offer training referrals, career counseling, job listings, labor market information, employment plan development, job clubs, and similar employment-related services.

> *You can find a center located near you by searching on the terms "Find an American Job Center."*

At the center you might investigate a job club or seek out a career coach or counselor. Employment counseling can help you to identify strengths and interests, set goals, identify resources, and locate training to better position you in the job market.

Many people found job counseling helpful. They were able to identify and find opportunities to upgrade their skills through training and education, as well as obtain financial support for the training. They expressed the need to be persistent and proactive in working with their counselor.

Employment counseling and job clubs are also viewed as sources of social support and encouragement. "It was a nice feeling to have people helping me and reassuring me," Kate said. "I have to say that the people I've had the pleasure of working with at the unemployment office have been very pleasant and supportive through this very stressful time."

Fend Off Age Discrimination

For many, diving into a job search after so many years felt like learning a foreign language. Helen, age 53, was married and held a bachelor's degree. She had previously worked as a laboratory technician for an environmental science company. The company reduced its workforce, and Helen was laid off. She had been unemployed for 17 months; she had received one month of severance and recently her unemployment benefits had ended. "I came to the One-Stop Job Center, and I asked to talk to a counselor," Helen said. "I think it was a good move for me because I had not searched for employment for more than 10 years. It's very difficult when you must compete with younger applicants and new technology."

Elena had been a résumé expert for her former company. Therefore, she was confident as she started her job search. "I knew from the start that I had a résumé better than 99.9% of the candidates out there," Elena said. "When I have interviewed, things go well, and yet I have not landed a job. I was a finalist in one process, and they offered the job to the other candidate. Now, I have only had two interviews since February and it's September." By then a certain suspicion had crept into her thinking. "I didn't think I was of an age where I would be discriminated against," she said. "I've changed my mind. I know my skills are great. My résumé is great. I do well in the interview, and yet I do not get the offers."

While many employers may not intend to discriminate

based on age, we know that it happens. According to a 2018 study by AARP,[1] 61% of respondents over the age of 45 reported having seen or experienced age discrimination in their careers. Discrimination in hiring does happen; it is also less visible and hard to prove. So, what can you do?

There are several steps you can take as a job seeker to set yourself up for success and reduce potential age bias from employers and recruiters. Start with your résumé.

Retool Your Résumé

Format your résumé appropriately. Make sure that it looks professional, that it is crisp and inviting to read. If you're unsure of what a modern professional résumé looks like, you can start by browsing free templates on Indeed or check with the local job center. Get rid of those graduation dates in your education section. Simply list the schools, course of study, and any achievements or awards. Consider using a current email domain as opposed to platforms that were popular when email was first adopted, such as AOL or Hotmail. Be sure to include only one phone number, preferably a reliable mobile number with a brief, professional personal voicemail message.

Keep your professional experience recent. While you may have 25 years of experience, the inclusion of jobs older than 15 years may distract employers from your skills and qualifications and may give your age away. If you have relevant experience from before that time, consider covering it in your skills or qualifications section where no date is needed. Your most recent jobs should command the most detail, with five to seven descriptive bullets. The rest of your jobs should only have two to four bullets. Remember to describe the impact you were able to make at each of your jobs, too.

Find the Right Company

You may have preferences for the type of company or organization that you are hoping to land a job with. Items such as company values, salary, and benefits may be on the top of your list, along with the kind of job and responsibilities. If you are a more mature job seeker, you might add age diversity. Pay attention to the age range of the workforce when you visit an organization. In addition, networking is a great way to unearth the culture of an organization and whether they are committed to an age-diverse workforce.

Check out the list of employers who've signed the AARP Employer Pledge indicating that they value the benefits that come with age and are looking for experienced workers. The list can be found at www.aarp.org/work/job-search/job-seeker/.

Look to see if employers have the AARP Employer Pledge Signer Seal on their company website. Another way to size up the employer is by paying attention to the language the employer uses throughout the hiring process, starting with the job posting. Look out for phrases like "high energy," "digital native," and "guru." Language such as this might be an indicator that they are on the hunt for younger workers. Look for your sweet spot, where there is an overlap between companies that are friendlier to older workers and positions that match your skill set.

Stay Current on Trends and Technology

Older workers are often stereotyped as not being current or knowledgeable of the latest technologies. Get out in front of this by making sure you know how to use new technologies. Consider updating your technology skills with a certificate program. Make sure they show up in your résumé as well.

Cultivate an Appropriate and Active
Social Media Presence

Social media is a natural "go to" place for recruiters and hiring managers. Make sure you have a LinkedIn profile page with a professional photograph. Take the opportunity to post content on LinkedIn related to the work you are pursuing. If you have a Facebook or Twitter account, make sure that the image these platforms cast portray you favorably.

Once you have scheduled time to conduct your job search, checked out free employment counseling, and took steps to fight off age discrimination, then it is time to begin.

Seeking Work

You may have heard a thousand times that you need to make your job search your new full-time job. You have tried that, and you are still coming up short, while the financial pressures are mounting with each passing day. Rejections and challenges in the search process over the long-term duration of unemployment make for a very stressful experience. You never really know why a company passes over you. Besides your age, it could be a host of other factors beyond your control.

"The pressure is mounting. There's a little bit of frustration building with the level of job that I'm trying to obtain," Lance said. "You're definitely overqualified for some positions, and you're not even getting looked at for *those* positions, let alone positions at the level you *are* qualified for." Lance added, "I don't mind taking a cut in pay. I don't mind taking a step down in role or something along that line. I'm just shocked that there's no consideration for you. I don't know what the reasons are, but you don't even get looked at." Coming up short in the job market, again and again, fretting about the reasons for being passed over for a job, and a willingness to accept a reduction in pay or position – all these circumstances characterized the normal job search experience for the people I spoke with.

So, what are some ways to endure the dismissals? Be persistent and carry on with your job search as if it was your "new occupation." On average, people I spoke with spent a minimum of five hours per day searching for work. Target your job search and set specific goals for the type of work you are seeking. Restrain yourself from applying to every and any job, as this does not make for a good use of time. In addition, make sure to leverage social media as well as personal and professional networks to search for work.

Regardless of the challenges associated with rejection and with not hearing back from potential employers, pit-bull determination must prevail. "No matter what, you have to keep at the job search," Lou, a former information technologist said. "You have to keep your skills sharp." And Kate said, "I just started plugging away, looking for jobs. It is an everyday thing. You really must spend a lot of time at it, every day, all week long."

Pursue Training and Education

Another major component of the job search process includes continued education and learning. There are excellent resources available through employment centers. For many, this became a time to step back and identify additional skills and training that might be necessary to be competitive in the job market, or to make a shift in careers, or to simply keep one's skills current while searching for work.

Terry, age 50, was married and held a high school diploma. Terry had worked most of her life in the accounting field. She was initially laid off from her accounting job and had been subsequently reemployed as an assembly worker at a manufacturing company for about two years. Then she was laid off again. She reported being unemployed for 24 months and that her unemployment compensation had expired. Terry had interviewed for a part-time job and realized she was competing with college graduates. "I saw the light," she said. "I needed to get a college degree if I want a job interview." As a result, she had enrolled in an accounting program at the local community college. "I feel like I have hope for the future by completing an associate degree. It feels very good that I can pursue that dream."

Kate, the former retail worker, was laser-focused on the type of job she was seeking. "Unemployment has forced me to focus on finding a job that I enjoy. Since I graduated from college, my desire has been to work in the medical field, perhaps in a doctor's office or at a hospital. It's something that I have truly wanted for a long, long, time."

The unemployment office provided Kate with the opportunity to enroll in training which helped her gain the knowledge that she needed to work in a medical office. They also provided the financial support to do so. "Updating my skills is something that I had wanted to do for quite some time, but working full-time made it hard to do," Kate said. She enrolled in classes at a local nonprofit where she was able to update her Microsoft Office skills. "Going to classes got me out of the house, and I was able to be with people."

Seek out low or no-cost training programs such as LinkedIn Learning, or watching Ted Talks by world-renowned thinkers, or searching out free online courses from top universities with coursera.org or udemy.com or openculture.com or lifehack.org. In addition, take full advantage of education and training programs through the federal Workforce Innovation Opportunity Act's dislocated worker program and others.

As a result of the training, people expressed a new level of confidence, hope for the future, and the ability to expand their job search to positions they previously were not qualified for. "The training gives me confidence that I not only know enough skills to get these certifications, but I know I have it assimilated, that I can go to the workplace and start doing this stuff," Walter said. "If I didn't have that confidence, I'd be much worse off, especially psychologically. I would start losing hope."

In addition to formal training and education, many kept their skills current by reading professional periodicals, attending professional association meetings, applying their skills to help others, and taking online webinars. "I try to keep up on the professional front and stay in tune with what's going on. I get five or six different Smart Briefs for Professionals daily," Lance said. "And what they do is they provide articles on most recent events in the industry, and so I have one for CFOs, for executive technology professionals, for the securities industry, and others. I'll read them, try to keep up with updates, the latest changes to compliance, and all the rules."

Like Lance, Tzippora, a technical writer with a master's degree in geology, tapped into online webinars and online courses to expand her skill set. "The other thing I've done is that I go to these webinars online. Some of them are in my field; I go to the ones on technical writing and new developments in the field," Tzippora said. "Content management systems are a big thing right now. I am trying to broaden my skills. I just found a grant writing course. It's very basic but that would be another skill I could learn."

Kate, who had previously worked as a customer service representative for a retail business, said, "My friend that I grew up with, she'll say, 'Kate, you've just got to take a break and just go out, take a walk, do something. You can't just sit in that room all the time. It's not good for you.' So, some days I might take a ten- or fifteen-minute walk just to get outside or go feed the fish." Taking a break from the search for work can help to maintain a positive mindset. Tom, the former telecom manager, said, "Take a couple days off, I mean, literally just go somewhere else to help reinvigorate yourself and get yourself back on track."

In addition to these tips, it is important to take the time each day to pause and reflect on what you accomplished and the progress you made. Celebrate the small wins each day.

The experience of Kate and Tom underscores a critical point – take a break. Many people described the importance of stepping away from their job search to rejuvenate and pursue an activity they enjoyed and valued. Balancing time between job search-related activities and non-search activities proved to be critical to maintaining a positive outlook during a long and dragged-out job search.

The key is to be proactive in your search for work. Access employment counseling, target your job search, refresh your résumé, and seek out ways to continue to learn and enhance various forms of expertise. Strive to gain new skills to enhance your competitive position in the job market. Pursue additional education and training — both formal and informal. It helps to stave off the unemployment blues and brings a sense of accomplishment. It also builds confidence. These actions demonstrate drive and initiative to a future employer and may open doors to additional career pursuits not previously thought possible.

Act Now!

✓ Approach the search for work as if it was your full-time job.

✓ Take proactive steps to fend off age discrimination.

✓ Seek out low or no-cost employment counseling and training programs at your local job center.

✓ Keep learning.

✓ Join a job club, attend a job fair, and network.

✓ Build in breaks during your day and don't be afraid to take a day off from searching for work.

4. Slash Your Budget

Conserve
Resources

It was the Thursday before Columbus Day weekend and the town of Warner was abuzz as volunteers readied the community for the Warner Fall Foliage Festival, an annual event since 1947. Locals and out-of-staters would enjoy the vibrant autumn colors along with arts and crafts, agricultural events, food, people, and plenty of entertainment. Even some of the residents of Pine Rock Manor, a long-term care facility in Warner, would be looking forward to their annual outing and the festivities.

Kate and I had decided to meet at the coffee shop on Main Street in Warner, a convenient and familiar place for both of us. I arrived early to secure a table and seats, and I found a nice quiet corner table at street level with a window facing the side street.

Kate arrived just after I took my seat. She smiled as she joined me at the table. Kate was divorced and single. She had been living in her own home, a large historic colonial, until she was stunned by job loss. Kate had previously worked about five years, full-time, as a customer service representative in retail. The company restructured and Kate had been laid off. When I spoke to her she had been unemployed for nine months and she was slowly coming to grips with being out of work for the long haul.

A bubbly, young waitress soon arrived to take our coffee order. We relaxed into our little corner of the vibrant coffee shop, and I asked Kate to describe how she had adjusted to being unemployed. As her voice faded a bit, she said, "The past week has been particularly difficult. I've been on a few interviews but have had no luck yet. The job situation out there is so bad. It's hard. There's nothing. Within the past month, I've been feeling really worn down, with all the failed job searches, the stress, worry, and everything. It's caused me to have stomach issues. I'm finding that it just gets so frustrating. I feel like I'm getting very drained and tired. It's exhausting, I think, because of the stress that continues every single day and month. It just really kind of wears on you."

Kate had held off on telling her parents that she was unemployed. "They're older and have had health issues. I just didn't want to upset them," she said. Just after Kate was laid off, her father had a mild stroke while her mother was in the hospital having knee replacement surgery. Her father ended up having emergency surgery at the same time her mother was in a rehabilitation facility for her knee. "When they were released from the hospital, I looked after them during the day. I worked on the computer and searched out available jobs to apply for. They eventually regained their strength and I remained unemployed, so I had to tell them about my situation, too."

Persistent worry and fear about her financial resources consumed Kate. "Wondering how I was going to pay my bills terrified me," Kate said. "I was able to move out of my home and rent a room from my friend. We are out in the country, and it's just very quiet and calm. That was a huge relief to me. It helped me to make ends meet financially." To preserve her financial health, Kate reduced her living expenses and slashed her budget, two very important strategies.

Kate also had found a part-time job as a receptionist at a local nursing home that specialized in dementia care. She worked 20 hours per week. "It was a good thing that I had this part-time job to demonstrate to potential employers that I was working," Kate said. "I enjoy working there. Being able to talk with my office manager and the residents of the nursing home

Getting Back to Work

and patients in the rehab center has helped me. It would be hard, I believe, if I was sitting home every single day dwelling on this, you know. And the income really helps as well."

You may find yourself, like Kate, without a significant other or a nest egg to fall back on during unemployment. In 2020, survey data from Morning Consult[1] indicated that 18% of U.S. households earning less than $50,000 a year have no savings at all to fall back on if one adult loses their job. And one in three (34%) would run out of savings after three months. John underscored this reality. He was a union industrial electrician and had been without work for 24 months. "I think maybe I've been extremely private in not sharing exactly how terrible the situation actually is when you have no income or very little income," John said. "You struggle to pay the bills and avoid being evicted." John was not alone in this battle. Anna, an aspiring artist, said, "I have no retirement accounts left. I had to cash everything out. I don't have anything. Our savings went to pay for my medical expenses." How do you manage financial stress and adjust to living on a limited income?

Unemployment benefits do not provide sufficient funds," John said. "I live rather frugally. I try to cover the necessities such as shelter, food, and keep the phone, electricity, and gas on. It becomes a matter of robbing Peter to pay Paul." Modifying your lifestyle and spending to accommodate a reduced level of income is the first line of defense. Regardless of where you find yourself, there are some immediate steps that can be taken to preserve what resources you might have or to help you stay afloat from day-to-day.

Identify Needs Versus Wants

Distinguishing between absolute necessities and things that would be nice to have is a strategy to maximize limited resources.

"As far as making any big purchases, I'm agonizing over even things that I think I could buy that might help my education, self-teaching stuff, because I don't need them now," Walter said. "I have to need it before I'll put the money out."

Deferring purchases can be excruciating, demanding, and cause tensions with loved ones. "At the grocery store with my family, if we're going to buy something, I question it," Anna said. "Do we really need it? If not, then we put it back on the shelf. And then we get into little spats over the money."

Lou and his wife were forced to set aside their aspirations. "We wanted to get a new, smaller car. My vehicle is a 10-year-old Dodge Intrepid," Lou said. "That's obviously on hold. We wanted to do more traveling too. Dreams are pushed aside, and there's nothing you can do about it. We're just trying to get by on my wife's paycheck and make ends meet."

Tzippora often settled for what she might have left in her pantry. "I will sometimes go a couple of weeks without going to the grocery store," Tzippora said. "I'm not fussy about food. So, I can be creative and try to use what I have."

Ultimately it came down to how best to cut back expenses or go without something. "Can I get away without buying gas today? Can I consolidate some of my errands so I'm not using so much gas? The other thing I changed is my shopping habits," Tzippora said. "When I was employed, I might stop at several stores for personal and household items. Now the only stores I visit on a regular basis are the food store and the drug store. I constantly put off purchases. For me, understanding want versus need is important."

Adjust Your Budget

Recalibrate and slash your budget immediately to help stretch your unemployment income and any savings or nest egg you may have. Try to find lower cost alternatives for the necessary items. Take a hard look at every expense you have with an eye to eliminating the cost or reducing the cost to the bare minimum. Some areas to consider follow.

If you still have a **landline,** consider eliminating it. There are many free Internet phone call apps available such as Google Voice, Skype, WhatsApp, Facebook Messenger, and the like. These apps let you make free Wi-Fi calls all around the world. (Preserve the minutes you have on your mobile phone for emergency purposes.) Most free Internet phone services can't be used to make a 911 or similar emergency calls.

While you are in the business of reducing your telephone expenses, don't forget to check in with your **mobile phone carrier** to determine if there is a more cost-effective plan for your household, or consider sharing a plan with friends or family members.

Check your **cable/satellite services** and try to reduce it to the most basic package for channels and internet. Reduce streaming services costs, too (Netflix, Hulu, etc.). Check with **utility providers** such as gas, electric, and propane to see if they can put you on a payment plan and work with you.

If you had **health insurance** through your employer, you will need to find alternative coverage. It is critical to insure yourself against a major illness or accident that could result in incurring major medical debt. Start the research at healthcare.gov to investigate options.

You also might want to explore a six-month or 12-month policy, in the event you land a job or your circumstances change.

Renegotiate and Restructure Debt

Create a list of all your outstanding debt, home mortgage, student loans, credit cards, home equity lines of credit, etc. Note the monthly payment and make a call list. Start from the top and work your way through the list. Explain your circumstance and how important it is to you, and to your credit rating, to stay current on your payments. Explore whether you can negotiate a lower monthly payment for a period or skip a payment.

Seek Financial Assistance

Immediately file for unemployment, and work with an unemployment counselor to identify and access available public programs such as fuel and utility assistance, food pantries, food stamps, and housing assistance that you might be eligible for.

"I've never had to navigate this situation or think about whether I should consider food stamps. Should I consider fuel/utility assistance?" Tzippora, a technical writer, said. "It's never gotten so bad. This is the new horizon that I am facing. There's the prospect of foreclosure. Do I want to let that just happen if I can avoid it? I want to conserve the little bit of money that I've got left."

Work Part-time

By working part-time while searching for work, you will be able to supplement your income, have something to do outside the home, and feel productive. What's more, potential employers will view you more favorably because you are employed. Pablo, age 52, was single and held a bachelor's degree. When I spoke to Pablo, he had been unemployed for 19 months. Pablo had worked as a technician at a television station for 26 years. He knew things were not going well financially for the station. "I assumed there would be some layoffs, and to be honest, if I was one of them, I would be okay with that because I knew I had a nice severance package coming," he said.

After three months of unemployment, Pablo obtained a part-time job editing newscast videotape for a different television station. He was considered a freelance employee and covered shifts as needed. He did not have any set hours or days and worked on average 20 hours a week. "If I were completely unemployed I'm sure it would have a big impact, but luckily my part-time job pays a decent wage rate," Pablo said. "I'm not making as much as I was making before, but I do okay. I've always lived very frugally anyway, so I don't need that much to get by."

Part-time work helps change the routine too. "When I started my part-time position, I had the feeling of shell-shock, so to speak," Kate said. "I came out of a cold work environment that was so stressful to this part-time position where people are nice, helpful, gracious, and grateful for what you do. It's really helped me. So, when I'm there it gets my mind off of things and I feel like I'm accomplishing something."

And part-time work can help fight off isolation. "If I didn't have this part-time job, I think I would be very discouraged about the future," Pablo said. "Just the part-time job really gives you a sense of purpose. The friendships and social interactions are very beneficial."

Reassess Living Arrangements

Adjusting your living arrangements, if possible, can help to reduce the financial strain. "I couldn't afford my house," Kate said. "My daughter and her husband, who were already living with me at the time, they took over my expenses for me. Otherwise, I'd be sunk right now. I was able to move out, and I'm just paying for a room from my friend. So just being able to pay for my room and trying to get by with the expenses has helped. My daughter really helped me out."

Anna and Lou also found themselves in a similar situation. Anna was able to find a win-win situation for her and her son. "My 27-year-old son's lease was up, and he was going to find another place to live," Anna said. "And I asked him to come and stay with us and help us out. It impacted our life significantly because we have a one-bedroom condo. He built a seven-foot by seven-foot canvas divider, which serves as an impromptu wall and as a canvas for my painting."

Lou had initially become unemployed while living in Connecticut in 2008. He eventually landed a temporary IT position in Portsmouth, New Hampshire, working for a large insurance company. During this time, he was able to live with his mother-in-law. At the end of six weeks, the assignment ended, and at the same time his benefits from Connecticut were exhausted. "We had spoken to my mother-in-law, and she had agreed that we could move in with her," Lou said. "My father-in-law had passed away, and she had been living alone in a large house in Portsmouth. We had nowhere to go at that point. I still had two children, who were in high school. They both found places to live with friends in Connecticut, so that they could finish high school."

You will want to be very thoughtful about the impacts, should you decide to alter your living arrangements. "We had three people living together, three different schedules, because my son gets up at three o'clock in the morning to go work at a pastry shop," Anna said. "He's got to be at work at 4:00 a.m., which means he goes to bed early. But we don't have a separate bedroom for him. My husband likes to stay up till 1:30 a.m., and I need to go to bed by 10:00 p.m. And then there's the dog."

Multigenerational households have become more common. According to a survey by the Pew Research Center,[2] three in ten parents of adult children report that the economy forced their grown child to move back in with them in the past few years.

To get by, you might consider renting a room, downsizing your apartment, having a child or friend move in with you, or selling your home.

Financial arrangements, household duties, shared spaces, and privacy are four critical areas to consider. Experts, such as Christina Newberry, author of *The Hands-On Guide to Surviving Adult Children Living at Home,*[3] advocate that people must be proactive and write everything down in an agreement. If you co-habitat under one roof, who will pay for what expenditures? What does a typical week look like? Consider meals, chores, TV use, appointments, music, pets, and social activities. Privacy is critical, says John Graham, coauthor of *Together Again: A Creative Guide to Successful Multigenerational Living.*[4] You will want to discuss how to ensure that you have a private place of your own to retreat to.

Try Bartering and Time Banking

Bartering can be a strategy to meet needs and spend less money. Elena tapped into bartering for a variety of items. "My doctor recommended that I get one of those light lamps for my vitamin D deficiency," Elena said. "It would have cost $200. There was no way I could pay that. I put the word out to my networks. And we bartered for the lamp. My husband found a cool gift for my gardening by bartering firewood."

Lou's hobby was photography. He found that it helped take his mind off his financial circumstances. Then his camera quit on him, and he was at a loss without it. "What I did is, I had been looking on eBay, and as a matter of fact, I found a camera very similar to mine," Lou said. "I am the high bidder. Financially you're doing that kind of thing."

Tzippora belonged to a religious community, and she has struggled to pay the dues. "I give them a token, literally a token payment every month," Tzippora said. "In exchange, I sit on a couple of committees. I write a monthly column in the bulletin too."

David Quilty[5] in Moneycrashers.com writes, "Bartering for goods and services is a centuries-old art." He explains that the idea of trading with your neighbors and within your community has recently received a big boost and taken on a modern spin. Combining our often-materialistic, ownership-based society with the internet's ability to bring buyers, sellers, and traders together, online bartering has sparked a wealth of new sites and communities. To help, Quilty compiled a list of over 30 websites designed to help with bartering.

Another consideration is time banking. Time banking is a time-based currency. Give one hour of service to another and receive one time credit. You can use the credits in turn to receive services, or you can donate them to others.

In his book, *No More Throw-Away People,* Edgar Cahn[6] listed five values that stand at the heart of successful time-banking and have stood the test of time.

1. **Asset:** Every one of us has something of value to share with someone else.

2. **Redefining Work:** There are some forms of work that money will not easily pay for, like building strong families, revitalizing neighborhoods, making democracy work, and advancing social justice. Time credits were designed to reward, recognize, and honor that work.

3. **Reciprocity:** The question: "How can I help you?" needs to change so we ask: "Will you help someone, too?" Paying

it forward ensures that, together, we help each other build the world we all will live in.

4. **Community/Social Networks:** Helping each other, we reweave communities of support, strength, and trust. Community is built by sinking roots, building trust, and creating networks.

5. **Respect:** The heart and soul of democracy lies in respect for others. We strive to respect where people are in the moment, not where we hope they will be at some future point.

Do you have items you are willing to part with that others may want? How about your skills and talents? Could you barter some of your possessions or your skills to acquire items you need to make ends meet?

Assess Your Timeline

Lastly, once you have put in place every budget reduction strategy you can think of, step back and take a hard look at your bare-bones monthly expenses. Look at your liquid resources, unemployment income, and any severance pay you may have, along with your minimum monthly expenses and calculate how many months you can go before you will need to tap into your nest egg, retirement savings, or be flat out of resources. Knowing that the liquid resources you have will enable you to survive one month, three months, six months, or a year, may help to reduce the anxiety and enable you to focus on your job search.

Act Now!

- ✓ Identify needs versus wants.

- ✓ Adjust your budget.

- ✓ Renegotiate and restructure debt.

- ✓ Seek out all forms of financial assistance.

- ✓ Work part-time.

- ✓ Turn a hobby into a paid venture.

- ✓ Reassess living arrangements.

- ✓ Try bartering or time-banking.

5. Balance Your Job Search with Meaningful Activities

Engage in Meaningful Activities

Rob had previously worked for 23 years as a printing press operator. He had always thought about making a change in his career, especially once his children were on their own. "But I was in a comfortable position," he said. "My job took care of my financial needs and more. And I created a niche for myself where I was in a glorious day-to-day environment. I was able to be creative, productive, and do it on my own terms without playing the games of the factory environment. I earned the trust of the people I worked for. I had a suspicion that when my kids became adults and finished college, I would make a change. I was surprised to see that I stuck with the career that I was in and never made the move."

Rob had a warm and gregarious smile. When I spoke with Rob, he had been unemployed for about nine months. "As the economy slowed, so did the printing business. I was laid off," he said. "And now I am reaching the end of my unemployment insurance payments." Rob was very self-aware and reflective about where he found himself in life. "I am full of questions and interesting thoughts. Because it's a whole new realm for me. I was in a financial situation where I could live all right. I had set up savings so that I could live the recommended eight months without pay. I'm also a hard worker. I don't like hanging around. So, I've earned money on the side. And it's all going well. So... the big questions are primarily related to my relationship with my wife."

Rob's posture shifted as he shared that his wife was challenged by the transition and adjustment to his part-time work status. She had grown accustomed to the comfort of Rob's career, which enabled her to spend time at home while they had raised their children, and then she worked part-time. Now all that was gone, and Rob was also working part-time. "She foresaw that the transition would be a challenge for her. And it is," Rob said. "The fact that I'm not bringing home insurance. The whole big package. Paid vacations. Money for savings. 401K. The whole thing was making her a very healthy, happy person. And now the challenge is for us to be equal. I'm working part-time. She's working part-time."

When I asked Rob about how he lived life differently now that he was unemployed, he said, "Almost no difference. My life is very similar, and I think a lot of that has been very intentional," Rob said. One difference was that Rob had more time for his hobbies, like riding his motorcycle and hiking. He had put these activities on the back burner when he was working. "I just dove into this motorcycle thing, and it's been enjoyable." Rob put over 20,000 miles on his motorcycle in leisure riding. In addition, he enjoyed working with rescue dogs that had behavioral issues. "I can only say that unemployment has absolutely benefited my quality of life. When I have self-doubt, I do more push-ups. I do more pull-ups. I clean the attic. I find these odd jobs for pay."

Rob had picked up some work on the side doing odd jobs and small construction projects. "I've painted a house for a friend. I've done a lot of cleaning jobs for older folks in the community." Rob reflected on his philosophy about unemployment. "I think you should stay invigorated throughout most days to get something done. And that hasn't changed for me."

Balancing Job Search with Other Productive Activities

Anna, the unemployed aluminum framing estimator, had been purposeful in her intention to end her job search each day with an activity that brought her pleasure and fed her soul. "What I'm also doing is I'm stopping. I am taking a break from searching for work," she said. "I'm doing my artwork. I'm getting out. I'm volunteering. I'm taking a day off and saying to my son, he's 27 years old, 'Come on, let's go down to the beach.' I have a right to have some enjoyment in life, even though I don't have a job."

Lou had previously worked as an information technologist at a national IT company for eight years. His primary job had been to interface with end users and provide software and hardware support. He had been unemployed for three years and five months. "You have to have the determination to find a job, to continue the job search," Lou said. "But you also have to have the sense enough to say, okay, I have to push away from this for a while, and then get back to it."

The constant rejection had been demoralizing for Lou. Day in and day out it eats away at a person's soul and self-esteem. How do you maintain hope? Keeping a balanced schedule lessens the negative impact of job loss and helps people manage the rejection that comes with looking for work. To feed their soul during such a dire time, many people I spoke with proportioned their time between searching for work and engaging in a range of meaningful activities including, but not limited to, household activities, hobbies, exercise, part-time work, and volunteering.

Household Work: Spending time tending to projects previously put off as well as household chores such as home maintenance, house cleaning, yard work, laundry, etc. provided another outlet and ameliorated the intensity of the job search. "Somedays I will prepare to tackle a small chore or a big chore, depending on what that is," Rob said. "I have multiple projects on my list to complete, such as house painting, rebuilding the deck, and cleaning up shelves in the basement."

And Elena, a former director of sales and marketing for a hiring agency, discussed how she and her husband refocused their energy on their home. "My husband and I decided to tackle some much overdue renovation projects at our home. We did the work ourselves, and that's been a godsend because I have done quite a bit of the work," she said. "I was dedicated to the work, sort of like a job every single day."

Hobbies and Side Hustles: Many people naturally enjoy hobbies such as art, painting, reading, singing, and dog training, yet rarely have the time to pursue these ventures when they work full-time. Pursuing a hobby or special project filled in the daily schedule in a way that mimicked the workday, provided a sense of accomplishment, and sometimes brought financial renumeration. "Something I always wanted to work on was my artwork," Anna said. "If you have a passion, something you love to do, if somebody's unemployed, they should be doing it, taking advantage of that time. They will be happier, and more content as a person, and therefore be able to think straight, and be better at solving problems."

A hobby can become a source of income too. "I've had dogs since I was age 14, and they have been a dominant force in my life," Rob said. He had some success with problem dogs over the years. As people learned about his availability, they started seeking him out to train their dogs. Slowly Rob began to turn his passion into paid work.

Do you have a craft that brings you joy and prompts family and friends to "ooh" and "aah" over your work? It may be time to think about your hobby as a business. Do your homework. Start by speaking to a Small Business Development Counselor or find a mentor through SCORE. SCORE is a nonprofit resource partner of the U.S. Small Business Development Administration. The mentoring services are free. They will help you set goals and provide guidance throughout the process.

Exercise and Self-nurture: Remy, 55, was married and had a high school diploma. She had previously worked at a family-owned woman's shop as a sales associate and beauty advisor. The shop closed, leaving Remy unemployed at the peak of the holiday season. "It's kind of nice in a sense to have more time to focus and to be outside," Remy said. "I have more interaction with nature by running, walking, and hiking."

According to the Mayo Clinic,[1] exercise improves mood, reduces anxiety, and may leave you feeling happier, since physical activity stimulates various brain chemicals. It also is known to boost energy and promote better sleep. "I make sure I'm exercising for exercise endorphins," Elena said. "I get outside and get sunlight."

Caring for and investing time in oneself had been important too. "The one thing that unemployment has helped me do is to become more conscious of my health," Lou said. "Not to say that I was a mess, but I was overweight. I've dropped about 15 pounds."

Opportunities to exercise are free or low cost. There is no need to join an expensive gym. Simply strap on a pair of walking shoes and take a stroll through your neighborhood. Find a free online class such as yoga. Check out your local community center for free exercise classes, walking groups, and more.

Exercise thwarts adverse health conditions and disease. Physical activity can also be a way to combat isolation by connecting with family or friends in a fun social setting or simply walking together.

Stay Curious and Current: A strategy many people built into their regular routine was to stay up-to-date on current affairs. Walter, the former telecommunications technician, retrieved his newspapers at 6:00 a.m. daily. "I read both papers, one for statewide news, and the *Boston Globe* for regional and national news," Walter said. "I also watch the local and national news each morning."

Pablo, who previously worked as a technician at a local television station, also used his time to keep up with the news and politics. "Well, like I said, I'm interested in politics and current events," Pablo said. "Listening to music is also a hobby of mine. So, I listen to the radio a lot. I'm either listening to NPR or I'm listening to a music station. Between the two, they keep me informed and entertained. To be honest, I really enjoy music, so just putting that on really brightens up my day."

Staying abreast of current affairs helped individuals avoid seeming out-of-date to potential employers or recruiters. Being informed about the world around them also made for good conversation starters, and helped people stay relevant. For those of you who stay in-the-know, keep it up. For those who don't, start. It will enrich your life, support your job search, and contribute to your general knowledge bank.

Reading was another strategy Walter credited with helping him get through unemployment. "I read something like a book or two a week. I also have several magazine subscriptions," Walter said. "Reading helps me to relax and set the worries of the day aside. My mind is engaged. It is good for my mental health."

Regular and varied reading is a self-development strategy. Helen Roots,[2] writing for the *Business Insider UK*, holds that reading makes you more attractive to potential employers. Reading can help you be more empathetic, build your vocabulary, strengthen your critical thinking skills, and enhance your own writing and creativity. Reading will also help you to switch off the daily stresses of your search for work, and to potentially sleep better.

Volunteer: Many found it gratifying to tap their skills to provide aid to another person. "Helping people who need assistance without pay is satisfying. The older folks think that I'm a young guy, and that my energy and diligence is marvelous," Rob said. "When volunteering to help the older folks with home maintenance, I see a humanness that's still left in these people who don't have a lot of vitality or energy. They're quieter, slower, less seen, and still utterly keen in their essence. It's been rewarding and utterly phenomenal for me."

Remy took her dog to the nursing home every week. It helped her to get out, work with her dog, and be with people. The socialization for the nursing home residents was a big plus too. "It's amazing what you learn from these individuals," Remy said. "Their stories are so impactful. You walk out, and go wow, what a great day. It really changes your perspective on life."

And the rewards of volunteering are not just emotional. "I volunteer to answer computer questions for friends and even for business associates," Lou said. "So, I'm trying to keep my skills fresh."

Volunteering pays dividends regardless of whether it is

working at a homeless shelter, serving on community boards, helping children, assisting older people, or any other volunteer opportunity. Strikingly, volunteering has been found to increase the odds of finding a job too! The Corporation for National and Community Service[3], a federal agency that promotes volunteerism, tracked more than 70,000 jobless people between 2002 and 2012 and found that those who volunteered had a 27% better chance of finding a job than those who didn't.

You may well feel that you can't volunteer your time because you need to be making money or searching for work. This is true but having another purpose and helping others will give you the energy and self-confidence you need to find a paying job. Volunteering also puts you into contact with a broad range of professionals. That network, as well as the experience you gain by volunteering, may turn into a paying job in time.

Consider what volunteering can offer you, such as new skills, building professional relationships, trying out a new career pursuit or contributing to a cause you believe in. Use the volunteer activities worksheet found at the end of the chapter and also available at www.kellyclarkauthor.com to help you sort through volunteer opportunities. Decide how much time you can dedicate to volunteer work and what type of commitment you can make. Think about what skills you have to offer an organization too.

Research opportunities with nonprofits in your area; check out food banks or historical associations or libraries that depend on volunteers. You can also search online through one of the following links or simply do an online search in your area.

- volunteermatch.org

- unitedway.org

- Engage.pointsoflight.org

- createthegood.aarp.org

- Redcross.org/volunteer

- habitat.org/volunteer

Give it a try. Don't worry if your first attempt is not a perfect fit for you. Keep trying opportunities that feed your passion and you will find a good match. Do not let the lack of pay discourage you. Reframe your thinking of volunteer work as unpaid labor to that which is a purpose-driven opportunity to continue being a productive citizen and a professional.

How will you use the gift of time productively? What tasks will you build into your schedule? What endeavors bring you joy and how will these activities find a place in your weekly schedule?

Act Now!

✓ Be intentional about balancing the time spent on job search and other activities.

✓ Take on a low or no-cost household project that has been on your list for years.

✓ Invest time in your hobby.

✓ Create an income stream from your hobby.

✓ Exercise and nurture yourself.

✓ Stay abreast of current affairs. Read and listen to free podcasts.

✓ Volunteer.

Volunteer Activities Worksheet

Action	Description	Notes
Decide	Decide on what you are passionate about. What do you care about?	
Identify	Identify what knowledge and skills do you have to offer?	
Determine	Determine how much time can you dedicate towards volunteering?	
Research	Research and investigate volunteer opportunities in your community? Inquire what friends and family members are doing?	

Utilize	Utilize online volunteer sites to expand your inquiry.	
Learn	Learn more about the organizations you are interested in. Find out what requirements they have, what skills are they looking for, what training and support is provided.	
Create	Create a volunteer resume or adjust your resume with the volunteer opportunity in mind.	
Act	Act Now! Reach out to the organization and talk with a volunteer manager about opportunities. Attend one of their activities, obtain a feel for the organization, and speak with the volunteers.	

Download this worksheet at
www.kellyclarkauthor.com

6. Access Social Support

Tzippora, who was in her late 50s, had been out-of-work for seven months, and this was not the first time she had been laid off. For a year and a half, she had worked from her home office as a contract writer for an IT company. "The company decided they would offshore the writing work, so they moved the work to Costa Rica and India, and then got rid of me and nine others," she said. Tzippora had over 20 years of experience as a technical writer. In addition, she held a bachelor's degree and master's degree in geology. She also had a certificate in software technical writing and a paralegal certificate.

Tzippora had other things on her mind at the time of the layoff. "I had breast cancer. I had just finished my radiation treatments the day after I had been laid off," she said. "My insurance ended within a couple of days which was the end of February." Tzippora had been unemployed several times over the last 10 years, and each time she was forced to draw down on her retirement savings. Now she had additional medical expenditures to cover. "I've now wiped out all my retirement savings and other resources. I will be out of funds in January because what I'm getting from unemployment barely covers the regular bills. And the money I've taken out of my retirement funds I'm using to pay the mortgage. Then there is my daughter's college tuition. If my credit rating goes down, that will impact her student loans."

Tzippora turned to cooking and baking for a reprieve from the day-to-day financial tensions, which was helpful. "I do all the cooking for family celebrations and holidays," she said. "When my daughter is home, I will try new recipes for soups and breads. It is a real treat for me to purchase a new cookbook, which is rare these days."

Tzippora received a mix of help and encouragement from her family. "My mom is my biggest supporter," Tzippora said. "She is 90 years old, and lives nearby me with my brother Alexander and his wife. Occasionally she will provide some financial support. However, she is on a budget too." Tzippora visited her mother every week, and she would call her several times during the week. "My brother Alexander and I have a difficult relationship," she said. "He would say things like, 'You're never going to get another job, you're too old.' Because he is family, his negativity has had a bigger impact on me." Even though her brother was so pessimistic, he still provided some financial support and assistance. "He is a mechanic," Tzippora said. "He takes care of all of my car maintenance, which is very helpful." Tzippora had a second brother, Xavier, who had also recently been laid off. "I am able to talk with Xavier," Tzippora said. "He understands and is more supportive." Finding people with common experiences to talk through is helpful.

Tzippora was an enthusiastic, life-long learner. Since January, she had been attending monthly personal development courses offered by Landmark Education. "The courses have really helped me," she said. "The simplest way to put it is that they make you think about your life, and what is bothering you, and then help you to work through situations so that you can move on without re-litigating the issue over and over again in your head." Tzippora had also enrolled in free journalism and blogging classes offered by the Loeb School of Communications. "The writing is key for me," she said. "People do not think about technical writing as being creative, but I do. Creativity is important to me, whether that is through writing or cooking or through the two online blogs I have started."

Tzippora shared, "Surprisingly, this time around I've been way happier with myself and my life than I have been during previous bouts of unemployment." I asked why. Tzippora credited her personal development courses and the social network she had built. "Mahjong is a tile game similar to poker and has traditionally been played recreationally by Jewish women," she said. "Lots of times it's therapeutic because we sit and talk about our issues, and we problem-solve these issues among ourselves." Tzippora was also a member of a religious community that provided support. "It's like a gift to me because it's almost meditative when I'm at services," she said. "I talk to my rabbi now and then too; he's a good listener."

Tzippora tapped into a key strategy for safeguarding well-being – social support. Social relationships and supports are frequently disrupted when a job is lost. The lack of social support can lead to isolation, loneliness, and negative health effects. Many people, like Tzippora, accessed an assortment of social supports to moderate the impact of job loss. Let's look at the strategies Tzippora and others pursued.

General Support

General support included a range of tangible supports by family members, friends, and professionals. Tzippora turned to her religious or spiritual community for advice. "Between the health issues and the unemployment issues I was facing, my rabbi gave me the name of somebody to contact at the Jewish Federation," Tzippora said. "There's someone on staff who has been helping people through hard times." For people without a partner, family, or close friends, seeking support from a spiritual community or another organization is critical.

Kate, the former customer service representative, relied on friends. "With my friend that I rent a room from, I feel a little bit of security just knowing that there is someone that you can depend on, you can count on." General support also included help with offsetting household expenditures, providing information, and companionship. "My son, he is designing and printing my business cards," Rob, the former printing press operator, said. "The business cards are for the home repair business. Home maintenance, painting, and yard work."

Emotional Support

Emotional support refers to the expression of care and concern, reassurance, and being able to rely on and confide in a person. Tzippora spoke about emotional support provided by friends. "I have my mahjong group. They provide a lot of emotional support," Tzippora said. "It doesn't matter whether they can help me or not. It is just good to have them as a sounding board." Anna, the aspiring artist, said, "Susan, my friend, I turn to her for a lot of emotional support. I talk to her, and we have been emotionally supporting each other as we are both unemployed. I turn to her when I just need someone to listen."

Emotional support from family was equally critical. "My wife, I can talk to her and gain her support with my approach," Tom, the former telecom manager, said. "If I can obtain her input, understand what she's thinking, then that goes a long way towards the emotional support I need."

And Anna said, "I'm telling you if somebody doesn't have family support, they're going to just beat themselves up. I have a husband and children who care more about my mental health and my physical health than they do money."

Family remained an anchor for Kate, especially during the rough patches, like divorce and unemployment. "Once a week on Wednesday, all of my family gets together for a meal," she said. "I get to see my daughter, son-in-law, grandson, parents, and my brother and his family. It gives me a break from the worry for a short period of time, and I get to be with my family. That is the best. They're very important to me."

You might be reading this and thinking, "Well I don't have family to turn to." Jump on Meetup or NextDoor and get to know some new people who share similar interests. Get to know your neighbors. Try volunteering. By focusing on others, we focus less on ourselves. Seek out alternatives if the support is not readily available at home or within your immediate network.

Encouragement

Friends, family members, and others encourage people to further develop their talents, seek jobs, and to pursue their educational interests. "My family cheered me on," Anna said. "My three sons and my husband. If I didn't have their encouragement, I don't think I would have been able to make these transitions. They said: 'Hey. The Museum of Art has an artist critic group. Why don't you take your work down there?' They prodded me in a supportive way."

For others, the encouragement spurred them on to pursue a talent. "I've attained results with training challenging dogs with behavioral issues," Rob said. "I haven't been constructive in making the venture go forward. A friend of mine just said, 'I'm going to set something up with the public library so that you can start to promote your dog training work to the people in the community.'"

Heidi previously had worked in the financial services industry and had been unemployed for over a year. "Hang out with positive, action-based people, and you will be positive and action-based. I've learned that lesson well, and I practice it, and preach it. It's very helpful," Heidi said.

The Value of Networking

Tzippora attended several professional networking groups as part of her job search. "I have a friend and we ride-share so that we can attend networking groups," she said. "We go to one in Littleton, MA, and there is another one at Temple Emanuel in Andover, MA. The meetings are held once a month and they have been a source of support."

Lance, the former V.P. of finance and development, said, "The only changes I made is probably I'm exploiting past relationships more than I had nine months ago. I previously was very cautious about reaching out because I was afraid I was going to alienate somebody."

Most of the people I spoke with took steps to cultivate and create new relationships at a time when it would have been easy to isolate oneself. "I reached out and reconnected with somebody I knew at Digital. We've been going to networking groups together and we commiserate about our job search," Tzippora said. "I also just started my own networking group. People have been very interested, very excited about it. When they leave the meeting they would ask, 'When is the next one?' So, organizing and leading the networking group has been a source of support. The Landmark courses I have taken have created another community for me. They have been very supportive of me creating this new networking organization."

Anna pushed herself to re-engage with a community of artists. She said, "Going to the artist critics group just pushed me farther along with my artwork, and they all were very encouraging of me."

Each of these individuals took a risk and reached out to existing or new social networks. This can be a difficult first step, especially if you are accustomed to being the one who has provided the support to others in the past. So how can you take that first step?

Everyone tires of making lists but they can be a helpful tool. The Canadian Mental Health Association[1] developed a list of the simple ways you can improve your social network. They advocate that you plan and figure out what support you need and then think through how you might find the people you need. Here are some of their recommendations to improve your social network.

How to Improve Your Social Network

- **Acquire more from the support you have.** Tap into your existing network.

- **Create opportunities to meet new people.** Strike up conversations.

- **Be a joiner.** Join a book group, hiking club, volunteer, etc.

- **Be patient.** Making new connections can take time.

- **Avoid negative relationships.** Surround yourself with positive people.

- **Take care of your relationships.** Keep in touch with people and follow up.

In addition to the tips provided, you can start at a very practical level by simply reflecting on the people in your network: those closest to you, and those who might be a bit more distant. Think about family, friends, neighbors, individuals in any groups you might belong to, like a walking group, book club, or exercise group. Then make a list of what you are most in need of in terms of support. Try to make a match between someone on your list and one of your needs that they might be able to help you with.

Next, make a commitment to connect or reconnect with three people on your list in the next 30 days who might provide support related to your most pressing needs. Be specific about when and how you will connect and the purpose of the call. If it is someone you have not spoken to for a while, then perhaps you start by rebuilding the connection with a call or email. If it is someone you know well, then you may be able to focus on the kind of support this individual could help with. Get started and commit to follow-through!

Act Now!

✓ Tap into organizations you are involved in.

✓ Cultivate existing relationships.

✓ Establish new relationships.

✓ Seek out positive, action-based people to surround yourself with.

✓ Avoid negative people.

✓ Make a list of three new people to connect with in the next week.

Resources

Worksheet to assist with identifying social supports in your life provided by **TherapistAid.com**:

See www.therapistaid.com/worksheets/social-support.pdf

7. Build Mental Strength

"You have power over your mind — not outside events. Realize this, and you will find strength."

— Marcus Aurelius

Build Mental Strength

Mental strength is the skill of reframing negative thoughts and adverse events. It is a form of emotional resiliency, which is the ability to cope with stress and challenges in a way that maintains our well-being.

Developing mental strength helps us resist paralysis and push back against the forces of fear and anxiety. When we build mental strength, we are better able to reframe the anxiety and bounce back from adversity. That is exactly the approach John had taken when his mental strength was tested by a lack of work.

John was a member of the International Brotherhood of Electrical Workers or IBEW Local 40. When we met, he had just graduated from Southern New Hampshire University with high honors. John said. "I plan to continue my education so that I can obtain a bachelor's degree in business management or project management." His enthusiasm was contagious.

John was a union industrial and nuclear electrician. He had over 30 years in the construction field. He held advanced security clearances, which meant that he did not need to go through Homeland Security and FBI background checks for individual jobs. At the time I spoke with John, he had been unemployed for 24 months. On the day I spoke to him, he had been hired to start a short-term job at Seabrook Nuclear Power

Plant on a scheduled upgrade. The job would provide a couple months of temporary employment. "I have experienced periods of unemployment in the past," John said. "Typically, I am back to full-time work within a week or two. It's not particularly the fact that I experience unemployment; it's the amount of time that I am now unemployed for." John added, "For the past several years I've spent more time unemployed as opposed to employed." Since 2007, John had worked in Maine, Kansas, Washington State, and New York. "So, it's not that I limited myself geographically," John said. "I would prefer to work in New Hampshire and be with my family, especially with my wife's failing health. However, I must do what I can do to take care of the finances, and that requires taking work where the work is."

John's parents were retired. "My parents live on a fixed income, and they struggle to pay for their medication," John said. "They barely have enough resources to live on. In fact, they could probably use my help and I can't help them now." I asked John how the rest of his family were   coping with his job loss. John said, "I am not the only one experiencing the stress. Every member of my family is, which makes for exasperating interactions between my daughter, my wife, and me. In other ways, everybody realizes that it's a tight situation, so we pull together." John's grandson was approximately two years old and visited every weekend. "The only activity outside of trying to survive and go to school is watching my grandson. He is at a very fun age where he is starting to make sentences, curious about everything, and he is beginning to express his needs and ideas. So that brings me joy."

John chose his words carefully as he spoke about how he lives his life differently now. "I've downgraded my living conditions. My children are on their own, so I do not have to worry about the quality of the school system. I am probably paying as low of a rent as possible." He had fully exhausted his unemployment insurance checks. John paused for a moment. "My wife has been a cancer patient since the early 90s," he said. "Presently one of her treatments is $3,000 a shot, which is 12 weeks of treatment. The money just isn't there. My stress level has gone up even though I try to maintain a good attitude. It's still difficult. I mean, I'm used to being able to work and make sufficient funds to pay my bills."

John was politically active. "Quite a few of my State Representatives and Senators know me by first name," John said. "I am not shy about expressing to them how they should be representing me. I haven't been quite as active recently. I do not have the time or the money to pay for the gas to get to their offices or events. I like to buy American-made products. I believe in my neighbor having a job. I believe if I go to the local farm stand or store or local shop, that I am participating in the local economy and contributing to my neighbor having a job. So I try to do what I can locally."

With 30-plus years in the construction industry, John was looking to make a career transition. "My big goal is to have the ability to take on a construction project management position, which requires a bachelor's degree," John said. "Project management opens up the possibility of being a supervisor on a job site and coordinating the entire project." John applied for grants from the Workforce Investment Act's training fund to continue his education. "I was accepted to Southern New Hampshire University. It was walking distance from my house, so paying for gas was not an issue." He had completed his associate degree in business management and immediately had enrolled in the operations and project management bachelor's degree program. "I enjoy learning. It expands your understanding of the world, and hopefully I will also see positive financial benefits, too."

I asked John how he was dealing with this period of unemployment. "It's almost like doing a 12-step program. I've done everything that I can to stay positive," John said. "To allow negativity to enter my process, or to get angry or upset, only makes the situation more difficult. So, it's kind of like you must face piles of trials with smiles. You can only do the best you can do. And then you must congratulate yourself that you did as good as you could do."

As John spoke about how he was dealing with unemployment, the words of my father echoed in my ears. Whenever faced with a challenging task or disappointment, my father's mantra was "mind over matter." The wisdom of my father returned to me as people shared their stories of overcoming hardship by taking control of their mind and reframing the way they were looking at unemployment. Like John, people utilized several cognitive maneuvers or mental strategies to safeguard their well-being during unemployment. These included being self-aware, remaining optimistic, using reappraisal, reframing negative events, and shifting work-identity.

Self-Awareness

Understanding how your emotions and beliefs drive your thinking, influence your behavior, and affect your judgment will help you navigate the choppy waters of unemployment with regained confidence. Elena, the former sales and marketing representative, described being attentive to how close she was to a breaking point. "I think sometimes I do get more depressed. If I feel myself getting depressed, I try to engage more socially, and I try to exercise more," Elena said. "I do all the healthy things you're supposed to do, and it helps."

Elena was able to name her strong emotions, worries and negative beliefs, which made it easier for her to manage her emotions. She precisely defined her feelings and put them into words.

John's introspection helped him to take control and manage his emotions. He was able to fight off the feeling that he wasn't in control. Instead, he recognized what control resided in himself and acted on it. "It's finding that center, and that's the best place to work from," John said. "You have to have the ability to step back and evaluate a situation and not become so directly tied to the situation that you have blinders on." John added, "I'm still surviving. I'm still paying the bills. I'm still going forward, mostly with a smile on my face, even though it's sometimes difficult. I am not letting the situation control me. I am trying to function within the situation as best as I can. I've taken what could be, and has been, a really difficult situation that could really beat a person down, and I've taken it, and made as many positive advances within that situation as I possibly could. I don't think I could've applied myself in any better way under these conditions."

Others I spoke with utilized time for quiet self-examination. Lance, the former V.P. of finance and development, reflected on the insights he gained about himself that could be applied in the future. "I got caught up more in what I accomplished and provided to the organization rather than my relationship with my manager," Lance said. "I had dealt with three separate managers over a period of five years, and in reflection I didn't manage their perception of me well. I will need to be more aggressive at that in the future."

And Tom, who previously worked as a telecom manager, said, "I was trying to play the game and I was not good at it. Some of the tools I was using were not very effective, so that's why I've done a lot of reading around emotional intelligence recently."

And Anna, the aspiring artist, spoke more directly to the point. "Unemployment has really been an eye opener, difficult, but it's really done wonders for me to discover myself. And at my age, you know the way I look at it is, well, I suppose I could have gone all my life and never discovered myself." It is hard to wrap your head around taking time for self-discovery when you are feeling the stress of job loss and all the tensions which come with it – financial insecurity, anxiety, isolation, and not knowing what the next day will bring.

Optimism

When I met Terry, she had just turned 50. She was married and held a high school diploma. Terry had worked most of her life in the accounting field. She had been laid off from her accounting job several years ago and was subsequently reemployed through a temp agency as an assembly worker at a manufacturing company for about two years. Her recent layoff was abrupt. "I was working for a job agency, and it was just a quick phone call, and in fact they left a message on my answering machine," Terry said. She had been unemployed for two years and her unemployment benefits were exhausted.

Every day, Terry faithfully worked to maintain a positive outlook. "When I wake up in the morning, I have to purposefully find a happy place before I get out of bed," Terry said. "I appreciate everything people do for me, which gives me things to be grateful for. It helps me get to a positive place. There are some days where I must concentrate on relief and let myself off the hook and let others off the hook."

Terry was hopeful about the future. "My college degree is going to help me, and I feel overall I am going to be more valuable to the company I eventually work for," she said. "I want to be positive. I want to see that my past has brought me to where I am today. And today will bring me closer to an improved future."

Terry and others sought out the opportunity in the difficulty they faced. Tom, the former telecom manager, said, "I believe that long-term, in the next two or three years I'm going to be in a much better place than I was previously." Optimistic thinking was a resiliency skill that individuals applied to overcome adversity. "So hopefully at some point in time, either through efforts out of my control or efforts that I've done myself to make the situation better, I will reap the benefits," John said. "I mean the economy could get better. There could be a lot of work. Or the work picture could improve... I've opened up, expanded my employability, and continue to expand my employability."

Now, it is easy to be reading this and think, "Well these individuals had been born with optimism." And perhaps that is true. However, there are some practices that can be learned which can help. Harvey Deutschendorf, an emotional intelligence expert, author, and speaker offers some approaches. These are adapted from a *Fast Company* article titled, 7 *Habits that can help you become more optimistic.*[1] Give them a try!

1. Before going to sleep, consider what went well today. Before going to sleep, spend a few minutes reviewing everything that went right for you that day, even the small stuff. What did you enjoy? What went well? What put a smile on your face?

2. Start the day by focusing on goals and expectations. Spend some time at the beginning of the day reviewing your schedule for the day and envisioning what success might look like at the end of the day. What do you want to accomplish during the day? Envision it happening.

3. Record your daily progress – however incremental. Take note of your daily accomplishments. Note small wins. What have you learned? Where have you improved? Make a conscious effort to celebrate your progress.

4. Practice gratitude. Try keeping a daily gratitude journal or notebook. At the end of the day, simply record what you are thankful for. It could be arriving home safely, the greeting from your four-legged pal when you walk in the house, a walk on a quiet path, the smile from a stranger.

5. Seek solutions first. Optimists don't waste time looking for people to blame or stewing on the particulars of an issue. They immediately start hunting for solutions. Can you cultivate a habit of seeking solutions when challenges present themselves?

6. Surround yourself with optimists. Optimistic people don't have the time, energy, or inclination to spend time with naysayers and negative people. Find more positive-minded, motivated people to build or expand your network with. You will soon find that optimists attract other optimists, and those folks will offer you support and encouragement.

7. Learn your way forward. Make it a goal to learn at least one new thing every year. Not only does learning support us in our efforts to think more optimistically, it equips us with the actual skills we'll need to achieve our goals and take advantage of opportunities when they appear.

Cognitive Reappraisal

Douglas Abrams in *The Book of Joy*[2] discusses how the Aryans, a nomadic people who traveled by horse or ox-drawn carts, used the words *dukkha,* meaning bumpy ride, or *sukha,* meaning smooth ride, to describe their journey. He goes on to describe these terms as a metaphor for life.

Individuals I spoke with used reappraisal, or re-construed stressful events, to steady the bumpy ride. Reappraisal refers to cognitive approaches that change the meaning of a situation without changing it objectively. It's not denying the situation. It is turning a problem into an opportunity.

> *"What is suffering but a bumpy ride. Every life is rutted, and no one can avoid some inevitable bumps. Our mind is the axle that often determines whether we experience the ride as bumpy or smooth."*
>
> *-Douglas Abrams*

Reframing Negative Events

Anna discussed reframing her circumstance as she spoke about her passion for her artwork. "When I worked, I didn't have time to do artwork," Anna said. "I didn't have time to do anything. I didn't have a full life at all. Now I focus on the happy parts of unemployment." Anna added, "You must turn it around. So, I focus on the fact that I can do more with my art. And then out of that I might be able to sell something, or I feel more fulfilled. And when you feel more fulfilled, you're a happier person, you're a better worker, you're more productive, and you make a better impression when you go for an interview."

Like Anna, many people conveyed a rich description of the phenomenon of wresting value from job loss. Remy, a former sales associate said, "So it's all in...perspective and....it's not the end of the world. It's not. There are people that are in worse situations than me, and I am very blessed, and I'm very grateful for the opportunities. And if I lost my unemployment tomorrow, it's still not the end of the world, unless I make it the end of the world."

Remy and others drew upon a strategy advocated by the Dalai Lama and Desmond Tutu[3], who said, "You can think about others who are in a similar situation or perhaps even in a worse situation, but who have survived, even thrived. It does help quite a lot to see yourself as part of a greater whole."

Reframing Work Identity.

Work often defines our identity, and how we describe ourselves. "I mean I don't have the career I had," Anna said. "I'm hoping to eventually have an art career."

And Elena said, "I know how to do drywall now. I know how to do all these things that women don't do typically, and it's really made me feel empowered, and it's given me a feeling of accomplishment, and it's kept me from falling into the abyss."

Some people talked about how their work-identity shifted during unemployment as they learned new skills and prepared to make a career change. "Once the training is completed, I will obtain a second certification, and then I will be qualified for a wider variety of positions," Walter, the former telecom technician, said. "I will be trained in telephones and IT. I can work at a help desk; I can work at a company that repairs computers." Others chose to take the off-ramp from an intense "career track" to simply find a job that would pay the bills or enable them to pursue a passion.

"I always wanted to pursue the next position," Anna said. "What could I take on next? I was always wanting to move ahead, move ahead, in a very aggressive way. Now I see work as just an income to allow me to do what I really want to do. And that is it."

Reframing View of Self

People saw themselves in a different light because of being unemployed. "I've always been very independent," Tom said. "I used to make up my mind the way I wanted to. The difference is that I now listen to other people more. I seek out their opinions as opposed to tackling everything in isolation."

Tzippora, the technical writer, said, "I started the Landmark courses in January, and I've been able to...clean up a lot of personal stuff. And I really have been much happier, I haven't been as worried as I've been in the past when I've been unemployed. Obviously the circumstances haven't changed, something in me has changed."

How to Shift Perspective and Reframe Situations

Blaz Kos[4], who writes about data-driven personal development at AgileLeanLife.com, described the ABCDE formula for doing cognitive reframing on your own. He shares that the first step is to accurately account for how you see the event.
You do this by:

1. Writing an **Accurate** description of the event.

2. Describing your main **Beliefs** around the event that happened and your feelings.

3. Noting the **Consequences** of what happened interpreted through your beliefs.

4. Next up is the cognitive reframing. This is where you add **Dispute and Effective Change** to how you are viewing the situation.

5. **Dispute** is about challenging your thoughts and beliefs to see a more accurate picture.

6. Effect involves writing down the **final effect,** which should be a more accurate view of the situation with a narrative and a path forward. This final step is aimed at replacing the negative thoughts with more positive thoughts.

Here is a practical example of cognitive reframing:

- **Antecedent:** I was rejected for a job I really wanted.

- **Automatic belief:** I'm worthless and nobody will hire me.

- **Consequence:** Anger (75%), Depression (25%).

And now let's describe the same situation by doing cognitive reframing:

- **Antecedent:** I just lost a great job opportunity.

- **Belief after dispute:** It wasn't a good fit. A job is all about a two-way fit; I'm only one part of the equation. I am being re-directed to something better. This gives me insights into future jobs and work environments that might be a better fit.

- **Effect:** Now I can better prepare a list of five new job opportunities and apply. The new feelings present are Anger (20%), Depression (10%), Inspiration (70%).

In this example, there also needs to be follow-up which would include the development of a detailed plan for how to identify jobs which might be a better fit and how to gain insights to confirm your beliefs. And to take this another step, find someone to share the plan with who can be a sounding board and an accountability buddy.

So where will you start? What situations could benefit from reframing? Can you reframe rejection as being re-directed to something better?

Using Positive Mantra

A mantra is defined by the Merriam-Webster dictionary as a mystical formula of invocation. Mantra originated in Hindu and Buddhist religions as a word or sound repeated to aid in meditation or concentration. "And one of the things I've been doing is going to a healing circle," Tzippora said. "I was taught some mantras to chant; one of them is a healing one. One is like an anti-adversity one. And I've been running those through my mind a lot these past few weeks. It's helped me remain calm. It's given me an anchor in some ways."

Terry used positive affirmations to make an internal shift in perspective. "I want to make the decision to take steps towards being positive," Terry said. "There are some days when I just must concentrate, and tell myself, okay, my job today is to focus on hopefulness. My situation can be very demanding. I try to incorporate…thoughts of hopefulness. What would be positive things that I can think about, and be hopeful for?"

What affirmative inner messages might work for you? One place to start is to consider the *12 Awesome Mantras for Job-Seekers* posted on the blog site Rake[5]. The article advocates that mantras can increase confidence throughout the job search process. The following suggestions are offered as a place to start.

Mantras for Job Seekers

When You're Not Feeling So Confident:

- I will find a job.

- I don't have to be perfect to get hired.

- Action conquers fear.

Before the Interview:

- I will bring the best version of myself to this interview.

- I am qualified for this position.

- I will make strong eye contact, sit comfortably in the chair, and relax my breathing.

- Today is just one conversation in my career.

After the Interview:

- I did my best. I gave my all! Whatever happens was meant to be.

- I believe I am valuable and worthy, and a meaningful opportunity is coming to me soon. I am worthy of this!

While Networking:

- The next person I talk to could change my life.

- People want to know me as much as I want to know them.

- Networking is not schmoozing.

Try one of these out! Take notice and jot down what shifts occur in your thinking and outlook. And finally, keep in mind the advice of Thoreau: "As a single footstep will not make a path on the earth, so a single thought will not make a pathway in the mind. To make a deep physical path, we walk again and again. To make a deep mental path, we must think over and over the kind of thoughts we wish to dominate our lives."[6]

Act Now!

- ✓ Try out the 7 Habits that can help you become more optimistic.

- ✓ Use the ABCDE formula for doing cognitive reframing on your own.

- ✓ Test drive the 12 Awesome Mantras for JobSeekers.

Additional Reading

Bolman, L.G., Deal, T.E. (2014). *How great leaders think: the art of reframing*. San Francisco, CA: Jossey-Bass.

Deutschendorf, H. (2016). Seven habits that you become more optimistic. Retrieved from www.fastcompany.com/3055069/7-habits-that-can-help-you-become-more-optimistic

Lama, D. And Tutu, D. (2016). *The Book of Joy*. New York, NY: Penguin Random House

Kos, B. Cognitive Reframing Exercise byAgileLeanLife.com Retrieved from https://agileleanlife.com/cognitive-reframing

Kos, B. *Cognitive reframing - it's not about what happens to you, but how you frame it.* Retrieved from https://agileleanlife.com/cognitive-reframing

O'Meara, R. (2017). *Pause. Harnessing the life-changing power of giving yourself a break.* New York, NY: Penguin Random House

Napper, P. & Rao, A. (2019). *The power of agency.* New York, NY: St. Martin's Press.

Rake (2018). *12 Awesome Mantras for Job-Seekers.* Retrieved on June 2, 2019 from https://2 Awesome Mantras for https://medium.com/@getrake/12-awesome-mantras-for-job-seekers-e16a37580475

8. Take Charge

Build
Mental
Strength

I met Elena at the offices of a colleague who ran a small consulting firm conveniently located near Elena's home. Incidentally, a private employment agency had been co-located in the building where we met. Elena had been laid off by a similar agency.

I had not been to the offices in quite some time, so it took me a few minutes to orient myself. As I walked toward the building, my thoughts went to the warm, summer-like temperatures, which tempted me to meet outside. It was late September, and soon the colder weather would settle in for winter.

I entered a small reception area where Sally, an older woman, was sitting in an enclosed office with a sliding transaction window. She looked up from her work, slid open the window, and greeted me. Soon she came around the corner and walked me down the narrow hall to a small room. There was an old oak table and five chairs. A brick fireplace and hearth warmed the room along with the natural light from a single double-hung window. The room felt homey, and more like the setting for a fireside chat.

Elena had arrived at 1:30 p.m. and appeared a bit frazzled. Her deep blue eyes sparkled and brightened when she saw me in the reception area. "I thought I was going to be late. I had trouble finding the location. I am familiar with the area, and I never realized all these offices were located behind this old colonial." The blonde highlights in her brown, wavy, shoulder-length hair complemented her round face and sculpted cheekbones. Her skin was bronzed from the summer sun.

Elena had worked at various jobs since she was 14 years old. She had been brought up in a conservative family just 50 miles from Asheville, North Carolina, in a small community situated at the entrance to the Great Smoky National Park and the Cherokee Indian Reservation. "My folks had a parenting philosophy that took no prisoners," she said. "I was raised to be independent. I left home the day after I graduated from high school without any financial or emotional support." Elena went on to graduate from college with a bachelor's degree in business administration and marketing. She found that jobs came to her, and people sought her out. She had grown professionally over the years and had taken on more and more responsible positions as her career developed.

Elena chuckled. "I worked in the staffing industry, as director of sales and marketing, which makes unemployment ironic," she said. Elena had increased sales over her five-year tenure by 183%. The agency helped companies find employees and unfortunately, as the recession settled in, companies were not hiring. "The entire industry was just tanking," she said. "I was probably one of the highest-paid employees in the company, which was like a big target on my back. I knew they were going to lay me off."

It had been a Friday and Elena had brought in a small gift for her boss, who was a new grandfather. "When I took the gift to him that morning, he nearly threw it back at me. He would not let me give him the gift," she said. "I thought, 'Today is the day. He can't take a gift from me because he feels so guilty.' Next the owner of the company showed up, and they eventually sent the secretary out to ask me to come to his office to meet with him, and that was it."

Elena was provided with two weeks of severance pay, but the company failed to pay out a large commission for a major sale she made. "I had just made the biggest sale in the history of the company, and they laid me off, so they didn't have to pay me the commission," she said. "They cheated me out of any kind of reasonable severance." Her unemployment benefits had expired, and she was on the verge of tapping into her retirement funds. "So that was just the worst," she said. "But I have tried hard not to hold onto the anger. I am very sad about the situation, but I have started to move forward."

I asked her how she was dealing with unemployment. "At the time, I had mixed feelings because I had felt for a while that I was ready for a change. So, I wasn't entirely horrified," she said. "I knew the timing was terrible, given the recession, and the other side of me was very arrogant. I thought, 'I'm a great employee. I'm a great catch. I have great skills.' I was sure that the recession was sort of for other people, and that I would find work very shortly." Elena had been unemployed for 30 months when I spoke with her.

Elena talked about how her situation impacted her social connections, like with her book club. "We've been together for 14 years, and over time we have gotten to know one another," Elena said. "There are two of us who have been impacted by job loss. Everyone else is still working. Their lives have not changed, and they are moving forward, and saving for retirement. They are oblivious to our situation." Elena became a bit emotional. "Sometimes people act as if there's something wrong with you. There's a little taint that maybe you were not quite up to snuff performance-wise. Sometimes the two of us stayed after book club and talked about our situation. And I have sought out other people in my situation because they're a lot more supportive and sympathetic." Opportunities to connect to and provide peer support to each other is critical. Unemployed individuals, especially people who had been in a job for many years, may have limited exposure to networks beyond their former employer and are at risk of feeling isolated and distressed.

Elena also found support in her family. "I wasn't close to my parents, and yet they have been supportive in their way," Elena said. "They are coming to New Hampshire for a visit in October, and they offered to have me drive back with them so that I could visit home. They also said they would pay my airfare to return to New Hampshire." As a result of being unemployed, Elena has related to her son differently too. "He graduated from college, and had been looking for work, so we were able to share notes about searching for jobs and resumes. He is a sound engineer and landed a job in the record industry."

Elena made an intentional effort to stay engaged and productive. She and her husband completed needed repairs to their home which they had put off for years. "I know how to do drywall now," Elena said. "I know how to do all these things that women typically don't do, and it's made me feel empowered, and it's given me a feeling of accomplishment. It's kept me from falling into the abyss." Also, Elena has updated her computer skills and completed a project management certificate program. "Sometimes I think of it more like a cycle. You go through cycles just like mourning. You go through stages. First, you're shocked, and then you're angry, and then you're resigned, and then you act."

Personal Agency

Elena's vignette illustrates the many ways she exercised personal agency. She asserted herself and took the initiative to influence events. People I met, like Elena, were proactive rather than passive victims of their unfortunate circumstances. Anna, the aspiring artist, said, "My family said, 'Hey, Portsmouth Museum of Art has an artist critic group. Why don't you take your work down there?' I wouldn't do it.... One day I finally said to myself, 'What are you afraid of? If you don't take steps and get out there you'll just end up staying in this cocoon. You're never going to get better, and you're never going to get a job unless you start having a different mindset.' So, I went down. It turned out to be the best thing I ever did."

Tzippora was frustrated with some of the networking groups and job clubs. "I decided I would start a networking group because I hadn't been to one that met all my needs," Tzippora said. "Most networking groups are just unemployed people sitting around and bitching, pardon my French. That doesn't get you anywhere. You need to meet employed people; you need to meet employers. So that's the difference with this group I've started."

Paul Napper, Psy.D. and Anthony Rao, Ph.D. in *The Power of Agency*[1] describe the ability to pause-evaluate-act as agency. They put together a six-step model drawn from best practices on decision-making to help catalyze change. The model is presented here for you to test and try.

Six-Step Model to Catalyze Change

1. **Pause.** Put yourself into a frame of mind and an environment conducive to reflection and exploration. Identify nagging or recurring issues that are coming up for you. Are you having trouble getting that first interview? Have you made it to the finalist round in several interviews only to have the job go to another candidate? Are your finances putting pressure on your relationships?

2. **Focus, define, and deploy.** Focus on the issue at hand to adequately define and frame it. Deploy critical thinking to test out your assumptions. Start to describe the scope of the issue. Put a name to the challenge. Commit the description to writing.

3. **Generate options.** Allow conflicting ideas to surface as you generate options to address the issue at hand. Test them out with trusted confidantes and friends. Withhold judgment.

4. **Manage emotions.** Notice and jot down the emotions that come up for you as you are reflecting on each option. Resist either-or thinking.

5. **Draft a plan.** Write your thoughts down. Describe the option you will pursue at this time and some initial steps. Create some benchmarks to reassess and a timeline to implement.

6. **Take action.** Take the first step toward implementing your plan, assess as you go, and make any necessary changes.

Once you have a plan, find someone you trust to share it with, and talk with them about being your accountability buddy, or find someone you can regularly check-in with to report on how you are doing with implementing your plan.

Be a Learner

Expanding your knowledge and capabilities and being open to new ideas helped people manage through unemployment. Tzippora conveyed a lifelong learning philosophy, "I'm always willing to learn," Tzippora said. "I've never stopped learning. I am a lifelong learner. So that's sort of what's been behind going to the Loeb School and learning grant writing. Just...trying to get some more tools."

Learning new skills and being exposed to different thinking builds confidence in navigating uncharted waters, such as unemployment. People regained self-confidence in themselves by acquiring new skills. "Completing new certifications is giving me self-assurance," Walter, the former telecom technician, said.

> *Don't sit idle. Use the time out to learn new skills, pursue certification programs, and take advantage of online learning. There are inexpensive ways to enhance your skills. Check out LinkedIn Learning, YouTube, and MeetUp Groups.*

Determination

Several of the unemployed conveyed a sense of being determined to do or achieve something with firmness and purpose. Pablo, the television technician, was frustrated with the response from his unemployment counselor. "It's like...the woman who was supposed to be helping me get this training, she's not coming through," Pablo said. "So, I'm going to try to make it happen myself. I mean, I kind of set goals, and do what I need to do to make them happen to the extent that I can."

Lou, the information technologist, said, "It's repetitive, but with a job search like this, despite what you hear on the news, despite what you read, you cannot give up, because when you give up, that's it. I think it would be a very bad thing to do. You have to keep at it no matter what, and even if you feel like you're pushing a boulder uphill, you have to keep plugging away at it. You must keep your skills sharp."

Many of the people I spoke with echoed Lou's "can-do" attitude. They were unwavering in their actions, and strove valiantly in their job search, despite the obstacles and setbacks they encountered.

Don't Blame Yourself

Taking care not to blame oneself is equally important. "I'm probably a little more resilient than some people my age," Walter said. "I am a veteran, I was a highly valued worker who got recognition throughout the years, I know that it wasn't me, it was the economy, stupid."

Elena had taken a suite of Microsoft classes to brush up on her skills, and she had met a variety of people in the classes. "These guys were technical geniuses, but they never looked for work before, and their resumes were horrible," she said. "So, I helped them re-write their resumes. And I came to realize that it didn't matter if you were a technical expert or communications professional or what. All fields were suffering, and all levels of positions. It wasn't just me."

Remy, the former sales associate, attributed job loss to external factors. "When I lost my job, it was no fault of my own," Remy said. "The store that I worked for closed."

In the end, structural explanations for unemployment won out over individualistic self-blame. The narratives of the people I spoke with focused blame for unemployment on factors such as an economic downturn, layoff, business closure, or outsourcing. Negating self-blame neutralized stress and anxiety levels and improved well-being. If you happen to feel that job loss *was* attributed to your actions, then try to accept it and learn from the experience. Focus on what you do well, instead of your failures. This will help you grow and avoid the downward spiral.

Avoid Social Media Self-Sabotage

Social media use is pervasive and has a tremendous effect on interpersonal interactions. It also plays a role in determining your potential employment with a company.

Take care to ensure you use proper spelling and grammar in what you do post for the public eye. Proofreading all content before you post is critical, especially if a future employer happens to be looking at your Facebook feed. Keep your content clean, demonstrate intelligence, and be positive. Your future employed self will thank you!

Negative online comments will most certainly be a red flag to potential employers. Take care not to broadcast negative feelings or vent about a former employer. Same goes for making crazy political statements or talking about your health and well-being online.

Enhance Your Agency

Some specific approaches can be put in place to enhance agency, regardless of one's baseline. One recommendation is to start with the seven principles for building agency developed by Paul Napper, Psy, D. and Anthony Rao, Ph.D.[2] These are listed below for you.

The Seven Principles from *The Power of Agency*

1. Control Stimuli.

2. Surround Yourself with Empathetic and Open-Minded People.

3. Move Your Body and Take Care of Your Well-Being.

4. Position Yourself as a Learner.

5. Manage Your Emotions and Beliefs.

6. Learn to Access and Check Your Intuition.

7. Identify Option, Then Act.

Take the free assessment at:
www.powerofagency.com/agency.html
and try out some of the tips for developing your agency, take charge, and make note of what happens.

Act Now!

✓ Take the Six-Step Model to catalyze change.

✓ Utilize the free self-assessment and enhance your agency.

✓ Explore learning opportunities and free courses to develop your skills.

✓ Avoid social media self-sabotage.

Further Reading

Deutschendorf, H. (2016). "7 Habits That Can Help You Become More Optimistic." *Fast Company*. Retrieved from https://www.fastcompany.com/3055069/7-habits-that-can-help-you-become-more-optimistic?cid=search

Napper, P. & Rao, A. (2019). *The Power of Agency*. New York, NY: St. Martin's Press.

White, E. (2016). 55, *Underemployed and Faking Normal*. New York, NY: Simon & Schuster.

9. Piecing Your Well-Being Back Together

Like Anna, many people conveyed a rich description of the phenomenon of wresting value from job loss. Remy lived on a lake with her husband. A rail-trail runs adjacent to the lake, and you can walk on the trail to the nearby community. When I had suggested to Remy that we meet at the local coffee shop, she was thrilled. "The coffee shop is located directly off the rail-trail," Remy said. "I walk daily from the lake to town. It will be very easy for me to meet you there."

It was a cool, crisp, late September morning. I arrived early and found a semi-private table for two. There were a couple of retirees seated nearby, and they were talking quietly about local politics and the upcoming mayoral election in town.

I settled into my seat and kept an eye out for Remy. She had said that she would be in a red Patagonia fleece. I saw a flash of red as someone opened the door and made their way past the take-out line. I stood up and waved to her. She made her way to the table and placed her water bottle and small fanny pack down. "I already had my morning coffee, so I will wait to order coffee," Remy said in a soft voice. "It was a beautiful walk this morning. The early fog was hovering over the river, and the sun lit up the red maple trees. It is such a peaceful part of my daily routine."

Remy was athletic-looking. Her golden-brown hair, wavy and tied back into a ponytail, complemented her olive skin and narrow-set, hazel eyes. She appeared vibrant and youthful. Remy had previously worked at a family-owned women's shop as a sales associate and beauty advisor. "When I lost my job, it was no fault of my own," Remy said. "The store that I worked for closed after 100 years of being in business. It was such a loss to the community." Remy had been left unemployed at the peak of the holiday season. She took job loss in stride. "It's not the end of the world," Remy said. "We have no children, so it's just me, my husband, and our dog, Isabella. There are people that are in much worse situations than me, and I am very blessed. I was mortified in another way. I wondered what I was going to do."

Remy utilized five strategies to piece her well-being back together during unemployment.

Engage in Meaningful Activities

Engage in Meaningful Activities

Remy had worked in retail right out of high school for seven years. During this time, she ascended quickly into management roles. In her leisure time, she enjoyed spending time with her dogs. She was able to align her love for animals with her professional work when she went on to become a veterinary assistant for many years. "It was my passion," Remy said. "I loved working with the animals and interfacing with the customers." Remy eventually met her husband and relocated to start their life together.

Remy had taken a job as a sales associate at a popular, high-end, women's clothing shop. Over the years, Remy had grown bored with her job. On some level, she embraced the change brought on by unemployment, and the renewed energy that accompanied the start of a new chapter. She viewed this period of unemployment as an opportunity to make a change. "I want to go back into the veterinary field or some kind of an office position where I'm directly dealing with people, and involved in the operations," Remy said.

Remy thought she would find another position quickly, given the varied customer experience she had. "I thought I would find work sooner and I didn't." She experienced disappointment and rejection as she searched for work. "There were a couple times I felt rejected when I didn't get the interview; I just got a rejection letter," Remy said. "After one interview I was told that I would be called back to do a job shadow, which I was excited about. And then they called and said somebody else was hired. I eventually realized that the opportunity was not for me. So, I just let that go."

Remy had a high school diploma. "I wasn't ready for college when I was age 20 or even age 30," Remy said. "I was doing other things. Now, it has become a little depressing. I feared the questions in interviews about QuickBooks or Excel experience. It would make me sick. So, I came to realize that I needed to have more skills." Remy worked with an employment counselor at the one-stop unemployment center. She applied for financial help for the training through the state dislocated-worker program. "I found a program through the unemployment office. It's a program where you take some tests to identify your aptitudes and what training you might need. I was very nervous about the test. I stayed up at night thinking about it. In the end, I did okay, and that was a milestone."

---

*Staying productive during
unemployment helps to keep
your mind and skills sharp,
starves off isolation, serves your
overall well-being, and builds
confidence as you continue to
search for work.*

Remy completed all of the paperwork and researched educational programs. She decided to enroll in the office productivity program at John Mason Institute. "Now is my time. I am ready to move forward and continue my education. I will start with a certificate program and gain the Microsoft Office and QuickBooks skills I need to find a job. It's a new chapter for me. My family and friends are supportive, and that gives me confidence to say I'm 55 years old and I'm going to school. I'm going to learn. So, I'm excited."

Unemployment is unsettling, brings on anxiety, and can feel disastrous. It equally brings about the opportunity to grow and learn in ways that you might not have expected. Remy, and people like her, stayed productive during unemployment. They learned new skills, explored hobbies, started business ventures, pursued degrees, took care of their health, and volunteered.

Maintain a Structured Schedule

Remy no longer had to get up early to start her workday or to take the bus into town for her job. She could have easily slipped into a new pattern of sleeping in later and enjoying the leisure of not having a schedule. Remy did quite the opposite. She continued to get up at the same time as she did when she was working. She maintained the same routine, however filled the time differently.

She normally started her day early and blocked out time to exercise. Job search was the top priority. Remy mapped a schedule that had her working on her search for work in the morning. She worked in a lunch break and then clocked a few more hours of phone calls, filling out applications, and seeking out jobs online.

Remy discovered that she had more time to get outside and to exercise given that she no longer had the commute to and from work, "It's kind of nice in a sense to have more time to focus, to have more time to be outside in nature to enjoy running, walking, and hiking."

On the weekends, Remy took her dog, Isabella, to the nursing home each week. She started doing so as part of her visits with her mother, and then expanded the visits to include other residents. "I've been doing it almost a year, and that has changed my whole outlook," Remy said. "It wasn't financial, but I gave something back. And it's made me humble. I return home and say, 'Yeah, I can sit. I can stand. I can walk. I can talk.' So, part of this unemployment journey is realizing that I could sit home and mope, or I can do something that I love doing, which is being with my dog, Isabella."

Remy and her husband also started volunteering at the nursing home for holidays and special gatherings on Mother's Day and Father's Day. "My husband did part of the cooking with the staff, and I was a waitperson," Remy said. "You don't want people to be lonely. So, I would find people who were sitting by themselves, and I would join them and strike up a conversation.

A daily schedule provided Remy with structure and a sense of purpose. She was able to reflect on her accomplishments each day whether that be job search related or progress with her dog or a special conversation with one of the nursing home residents. Remy was intent on filling her schedule with meaningful activities.

Conserve Resources

Conserve
Resources

The threat posed by job loss to financial well-being can be overwhelming. The pressures brought on by the loss of income create tension and distress. Remy and the millions of unemployed people who are trying to figure out how to survive on a substantially reduced income know this all too well.

Remy had led a lifestyle where she had paid her bills and had saved money. She limited leisure spending to what resources were left over. "And if I don't have the money, then I'm not going to spend," Remy said. She was fortunate that her husband was self-employed and could pick up more of the household expenses. This left Remy feeling like she was not financially contributing. "In my head, it seemed like I was not contributing financially, when I actually am contributing through other things I do, such as cleaning and taking care of the house."

Remy had trained her dog, Isabella, by taking her down to the common in town, where they could work on socialization and commands in a distracted environment. This led to the start of a small business on the side to generate additional income. "I groom animals too. I've taught myself how to groom through all those years in the veterinary field," Remy said. "It brings in some revenue to offset our expenses and helps me feel like I am contributing a bit more."

Remy re-prioritized financial goals. She had been in the habit of helping others. "I try to help out my nieces and nephews because they are in their 30s, raising children, and they struggle from time to time." Remy said. "I've been in that situation, growing, and struggling, and trying to make a place in the world. Now, I must curtail my financial giving and I just wish I could help like I used to."

Finding ways to survive on limited resources helped to reduce anxiety over finances, as painful as it was to give so much up. People prioritized needs over wants. They adjusted their budgets, sought out assistance from family and friends, bartered, and, when necessary, reassessed their living situation.

Access Social Support

Activating social support networks to buffer the negative impacts of job loss, and to fight off isolation and loneliness is critical. Many people took a risk and created new social support networks to replace ones left behind at their former place of employment. Remy was no different. "I have a wide range of friends that I talk with, and they are positive," Remy said. "The relationships from work are gone, and I have made new friends. I'm not afraid to make new friends. You've got to put yourself out there. The support of my immediate family is also critical."

Remy sought out new relationships in a variety of places. "Going to the endodontist, I met the receptionist, and we have become friends, and we do things together," Remy said. "I get together with one of my former co-workers, and we have lunch once a month. Then there are the people in my condominium complex. They are all very supportive of my return to school, too." And then there was the walking club. "That is where I've met other people, some in their 70s and 80s," Remy said. "It has been a source of social support, just to talk with other people about their life experiences. I just have fun, and I enjoy their company. I've made new friends, and I have learned a lot about people in my community."

The unemployment counselors were also a source of social support for Remy. "I have had support through the unemployment office," Remy said. "The counselors have been very helpful. They don't look at me like I have three heads because I'm unemployed. They truly want to help you and support you in your search for a new job."

Build Mental Strength

Build
Mental
Strength

Emotional stress is unavoidable with job loss. Emotions can eat you up, or they can serve you. It all starts with being self-aware and then acting. Remy applied her own set of mind-set rules. She set an intention to stay positive. "So, it's all in perspective and it's not the end of the world," Remy said. "If I lost my unemployment payments tomorrow, it's still not the end of the world unless I make it the end of the world."

Remy was determined to find work. "It's going to happen. I am going to be employed," she said. "If I listen to the media, if I listen to all the negativity, then it's going to impact me, and I'm going to feel negative, and I'll be in a slump. I don't want to be that way. So, you say to yourself, 'I'm going back to school. I'm going to make this transition, and it's going to be a better one.' If I don't keep on that journey in my lifestyle and my mind, it's not going to happen."

Remy described having a belief in something bigger than herself. This belief or faith propelled her forward. "I have a sense of peace and comfort that all will be well," Remy said. "I credit my spirituality for this, and how I've chosen to look at things. Not in organized religion. My spirituality and people that have helped me through this journey."

Our mind is powerful. The ability to tune into your thoughts and expand your awareness around them is what Rachel O'Meare[1] described as "Mental Flossing." She advocates that you can consciously shift your behavior and move from a mindless "monkey-mind" mode to a more conscious way of thinking and acting. It is a chance to align with more intentional attitudes and beliefs, which lead to new behaviors and actions.

The Well-Being Framework

Remy's simultaneous application of the five strategies helped to safeguard her well-being and put the pieces back together while she explored and set a new course for herself. The positive benefits of the activities she pursued, such as socialization, self-care, training, and turning her hobby into a side-business, offset the tension and rejection that comes with searching for work.

The people I spoke with put the five strategies into action to maintain their well-being. They sought out emotional and social support from family and friends, and equally engaged in problem-solving activities like pursuing education and training, working part-time, pursuing a hobby, and finding a new job.

Anyone can apply this framework and the five strategies, like Remy, by using the tools covered in each chapter and summarized here. Remember, you can find all the tools mentioned in this book at www.kellyclarkauthor.com. Choose which strategies to start with and write one or two steps you will take and a time frame for doing so. You might start working on one task for one strategy or a suite of activities for a subset of strategies. Identify the activities that resonate most for you and try them for a week. Notice what shifts occur and what works for you. Keep the strategies that work, drop what doesn't, and add to your repertoire as you go. Maintain a journal or write down the shifts you experience and the changes you make. Finally, seek out someone you can confide in, someone who will hold you accountable, and share your approach with them. Establish a regular time to check in and discuss your progress.

What tools or strategies have helped you to maintain your well-being during employment? Share your experience and suggestions with others at the author's website: www.kellyclarkauthor.com

Closing

> *It is not the critic who counts; not the man who points out how the strong man stumbles, or where the doer of deeds could have done them better. The credit belongs to the man who is actually in the arena, whose face is marred by dust and sweat and blood; who strives valiantly; who errs, who comes short again and again, because there is no effort without error and shortcoming; but who does actually strive to do the deeds; who knows great enthusiasms, the great devotions; who spends himself in a worthy cause; who at the best knows in the end the triumph of high achievement, and who at the worst, if he fails, at least fails while daring greatly, so that his place shall never be with those cold and timid souls who neither know victory nor defeat.*

> *—Theodore Roosevelt*

As I reflected on the stories told by people experiencing unemployment, I was drawn again to this quote, which was taken from Theodore Roosevelt's 1910 speech, "The Man in the Arena." For me, the quote captures the grit, the emotion, and the resolve of the unemployed people I have met with. Their actions embodied the words of Roosevelt.

What we learned from their experience and journey through unemployment is how to "stay in the arena," and "fight the good fight," while taking care of yourself and your well-being – all of which supported their continued search for work and increased the odds of reemployment.

10. Where Are They Now?

It was autumn of 2020. The world had been in the middle of the COVID-19 pandemic. Racial injustice and tension permeated the United States, and the country was in turmoil over the upcoming Presidential election. I, like many Americans, had been adjusting to a new sort of virtual existence.

I was in the middle of writing this book and my mind frequently turned to the people who had shared their experiences with me. I wondered, how were they doing? What were they doing? Were they employed? What coping skills, in hindsight, had helped them most through unemployment? What follows are the stories of five people and where they ended up.

Uprooted & Resettled
Elena

Elena, the former director of sales and marketing for a staffing company, was the first person to respond to my inquiry. She was enthusiastic about speaking with me again. We agreed to meet virtually over Zoom. The format had not been a surprise, given the Zoom-heavy pandemic era. Elena had taken the Zoom call during her lunch break at work, seated at a desk facing the camera on her computer. Behind her was a familiar setting, which appeared to be a long-term care facility.

Elena's deep blue eyes lit up as we both appeared on video. "It is great to see you again," she said. "It is nice that you're doing these follow up discussions to see what happened to people." We exchanged greetings, discussed how we were dealing with COVID-19, and commented on how quickly time had passed since we spoke last. "I think I aged more physically, and with the stress of unemployment, I have put on weight and experienced sleep problems." Her brown hair with blonde highlights, worn shoulder-length with bangs, framed her rounded face and rosy cheeks. Elena was now in her late 50s.

Elena had reached a dead end with her search for work in New Hampshire. "I was completely incapable of finding a job," Elena said. "I could not even get an interview, and I had a killer resume." Elena's parents had lived in a small community near the Cherokee Indian Reservation in North Carolina. She had grown up in a very conservative household and her parents were religious. "It was my mother, which seems incredulous since my parents are anti-gambling. She had told me that construction had started on a new casino on the reservation, and that they were going to hire 400 people. It was a small town, and it was isolated, which meant that the casino would not have a large pool of people to hire from."

Elena had packed her bags and headed to North Carolina. Tom, her husband, had been employed as general contractor for over 14 years with the same company. Uncertain of Elena's work prospects, he had decided to stay behind in New England. Elena's parents welcomed her with open arms. She had moved in with her parents while she explored job opportunities at the casino. "I quickly learned that they needed card dealers. The pay was really good, and they sent all new dealers to school for five weeks." Elena applied for and was hired as a card dealer, contingent upon the successful completion of the course work and training.

Elena had only played cards maybe five times in her whole life. "I survived and I thrived," Elena said. "I am very proud of myself. I passed the class." Once she felt settled into her new job as a card dealer at the casino, she had started the search for a home. "We refinanced our house in New Hampshire and took the money to buy a house in North Carolina." Once Tom rented their house in New Hampshire, he left for North Carolina–unemployed and without a job prospect on the horizon. "He left a great job in New England to move to North Carolina," Elena said. "So, the stable employed person left his job. It was very risky, and he was older than me."

Elena eventually found a house with an in-law apartment. The house was a fixer-upper, but she had been confident in the skills she learned remodeling the New England house. For the first time in a very long time, Elena found comfort in her work colleagues. "I can't tell you how many recession refugees worked at the casino," Elena said. "There were so many ex-professionals working in the casino; you could have staffed an entire company with just the dealers on the casino floor. There were engineers, communications professionals, information technologists, and many more. Everyone was there because of the recession. They all had arrived there differently, but their story was very similar to my experience."

In New England, Elena had been suspicious about the challenges she encountered in finding work. "The casinos are probably the least discriminatory employers in the United States," Elena said. "The reason is that they want the card dealers to look like their customers. I felt like I was encountering ageism when I looked for work in New England, and the casino is the one place that is not like that."

Elena eventually moved on from dealing cards to become the marketing and events director, but eventually grew restless with her work at the casino. Elena and Tom had been living in North Carolina for over six years. "My husband was only going to tolerate being down South for so long," Elena said. "He is a true Yankee, and his experience of the South was not so favorable. So, I thought to myself, 'What job can I find that would be transferable back to New England?' I was not optimistic about the job market in New England, so I figured a transfer might be my best option."

A friend of Elena's back in New Hampshire informed her that a large investment company was planning to open a new office in Lebanon, New Hampshire. Elena researched the company in North Carolina and located an office in Asheville, North Carolina, which was a short drive from her home. "I applied for a job as a branch administrator. It was a lower-level position; however, you could transfer anywhere in the system. I accepted the position."

In the spring, Elena was able to transfer to the new branch in Lebanon. The timing was perfect. Tom secured work as a general contractor for the company he had previously worked for.

After a year or so, Elena had started to search for different work again. She was looking for a higher-level position and someplace where she could make a real contribution. "I found a position as an Executive Assistant to the CEO, CFO, and CIO at a hospital in the Upper Valley area of New Hampshire," Elena said. "The hospital cares for more than 20,000 patients per year, and there are 500 staff members. The pay was much better, and they immediately recognized my skill set. Shortly after I had started working at the hospital, I was given the responsibility for the contract management system too. I currently hold dual positions as the Executive Assistant and Contract Manager." Elena had finally settled back into a professional position in New Hampshire.

When I had previously spoken with Elena, she had described her aspiration to me. "My outlook is to find an employer that I can settle in with, and if I'm lucky, grow in place." Now, Elena reflected on her journey. "I'm finally in a place where I feel appreciated," Elena said. "I feel recognized. The pay is not at the level I was making before I was laid off, however, it is a livable wage, and I think my boss is grooming me to take her job when she retires. I am very hopeful for the future."

Picking up the Pieces

I asked Elena to reflect on her unemployment journey and to speak to what supports had been the most helpful to her. "The most instrumental support I received was from my husband and my parents," Elena said. "I would also note that the most supportive person throughout this experience has been my husband," Elena said. Unconditional support from loved ones was critical as was the reassurance from friends. "Reaching out and making a special effort to stay connected to friends was one of the most helpful actions that I took. Especially the friends that had similar experiences." Proactively nurturing her small circle of friends was difficult, given Elena's experience with her book club in 2011. "I lost a lot of faith in many of my friends who turned out not to be so supportive. They never reached out. They made me feel deficient because I was laid off. But the friends I stayed close to, the people going through unemployment, they are still my best friends today."

Determination, with firmness and purpose, was evident in Elena all these years later. "I stayed hopeful, and I never gave up on myself," Elena said. "I have a strong work ethic and self-identity. Unemployment helped me to realize that I am so much more as a person than just my work identity. I am more focused on spending time with my husband than I was back in 2011. I am not a career maniac, and my marriage has blossomed as a result."

Elena had made some calculated steps. "I am a very analytical person," Elena said. "I tried to play out the risk-benefit analysis, and not respond with emotion. That doesn't mean it wasn't difficult, there still was a huge emotional component. It had played out in sleepless nights, stress, and weight gain."

Identifying with others made a difference for Elena. "It wasn't just me that ended up unemployed," Elena said. "I had seen first-hand, with my casino colleagues, that so many people, especially in my age group had lost their jobs to the recession. It was helpful for me to know that I wasn't alone. It wasn't just me."

Financially, Elena had taken some losses over the years. "I went through a hunk of my retirement savings to make ends meet," Elena said. "That has been one of the worst parts and challenges, even today." The state of the economy in 2020 and the impacts of COVID-19 had added volatility to Elena's situation. "I needed some growth in my assets to retire," Elena said. "It is just not going to happen on the timetable I had initially planned, so I have had to adjust my expectations. It has been difficult to let go of that because it had been a dream, and plan, for so very long to retire early. I won't have to work until I'm age 80, but I will be working into my late 60s for sure."

As we closed out our conversation, Elena said, "It has been a very weird path and journey for me. Fortunately, it has all worked out. We are right back where we started, living on a small lake in New Hampshire, and hopeful about our future."

Re-employed & Retired
Walter

Walter joined the Zoom call from his home in northern New Hampshire. Over the years, he had balded and had grown a gray mustache and neatly shaved goatee. He wore black-rimmed glasses that complemented his round face, light complexion, and deep brown eyes. Walter had previously worked as a telecommunications technician. His home office featured oak posts and beams that were prominent against the off-white walls. Clouds and fog were visible through the two double-hung windows behind Walter. On the wall, vigilantly watching from high above the fireplace, three high-quality taxidermy mooseheads looked down over Walter. I commented that one of the three mooseheads on the wall looked to be from a good-sized moose. In a deep, husky voice, Walter said, "That's a redundant statement; moose are all good-sized. Even the small ones are big. The one in the center is from Ossipee, New Hampshire." His sense of humor and precision with words remained years later.

When I last spoke to Walter, he was finishing up his training. He had been upgrading his skills, from servicing telephone systems and circuits to learning internet protocol so that he could provide IT support. He had obtained one certificate to service personal computers, another for managing computer networks, which included training on routers and switches that connect the computer to the Internet, and a third focused on network security.

Walter had completed two of the three trainings when he was contacted by a military contractor who had learned of his expertise with telephone systems from a former colleague. The military contractor was looking to send someone with experience servicing the older telephone systems to Afghanistan. "They dangled a six-figure contract in front of me," Walter said. "Room and board would be included. A good portion of the income would be exempt from federal taxes. I just thought that if I took this job for a year, and banked most of the money, then the resources could hold me over until I would be eligible for Social Security." Walter's 80-year-old father begged him not to go. "My father offered to pay me what unemployment had been paying me. He had insisted that I turn the offer down."

Walter, being the skeptic and the detailed-oriented person

that he was, had done his homework. Several times, to no avail, he had requested a copy of the employment contract from the recruiter. "Finally, I searched out the recruiting company in Natick, Massachusetts," Walter said. "I had talked to an administrator in Human Resources. I had requested a copy of the contract, which she had sent me. Overseas military contractors were excluded from all of the liability and employment provisions. I would have nothing to fall back on if there was any wrong-doing. The contract was worthless."

One Friday night, when Walter was singing with his Irish music group, he met Gillian, a vice-president for human resources for a local manufacturing company. She had been singing with the group that night and had struck up a conversation with Walter. "I had learned about two I.T. support positions that Gillian's company was recruiting for," Walter said. "She encouraged me to apply for the higher-skilled position, even though I did not have the exact skill set."

Meanwhile, Walter was scheduled to leave in 10 days to attend an orientation for overseas contractors at Camp Atterbury in Indiana. "I thought long and hard about the overseas work," Walter said. "Ultimately, I turned the overseas job down. It was more risk than I was willing to take on. In hindsight, it was the right decision."

Walter had applied for two positions at the manufacturing company. He was invited in for two interviews and was offered a position providing call center support in the marketing department. "The job paid half of what I was making before I was laid off," Walter said. "The position provided benefits, and my commute was cut in half. So that made up for some of the difference." Walter provided IT support to 85 salespeople. Just as Walter had started to settle into his new job, his wife, Cara, faced some unsettling times. "My wife was laid off for about nine months," Walter said. "She eventually found another job through a colleague she had worked with."

The technical requirements of Walter's job morphed a couple of times. "I was moved from the sales department to the marketing department, and then eventually to the IT department," Walter said. "I had progressed in the organization, and eventually I was making the same pay as I had pre-unemployment." Walter and Cara had fallen back into their pre-unemployment routines, and they tried to catch up financially.

Walter worked six years with the manufacturing company. "I had been transferred to report to the vice-president, who was also the national call center director. He was in Los Angeles," Walter said. "I had never met him. I had no management support in my time zone. He would say, 'Call me anytime you need me.' But he wasn't very responsive, even with urgent requests. He had other irons in the fire in New York or New Jersey."

By July, things at work had reached a tipping point. "Four times I sent my boss an email noting that I needed a few minutes of his time," Walter said. "He would reply, 'I am swamped. I will get back to you.' He never got back to me over a four-month period." Walter and his wife, Cara, decided to meet with a financial advisor to determine the impact of Walter leaving his job.

Walter gave his notice to the manufacturing company in early August 2017. The Friday before Labor Day weekend was his last day of work. "I received 10 weeks of pay based on my time with the company," Walter said. "I was able to go on COBRA for insurance, and I had some vacation and floating personal days due to me. Financially this helped with the transition. Also, many of the strategies I had put in place when I had been laid off helped me to adjust to the psychological realization that my working days had come to an end."

Picking Up the Pieces

Walter had lived frugally. "We had very little debt," Walter said. "Our mortgage had been the biggest concern." Walter had savings to fall back on, unemployment payments, and his wife was working. "I was never really stressed until right up near the end, the 53rd week, when my unemployment was running out," Walter said. "I had turned down the Afghanistan contract, I wasn't willing to accept my father's financial help, and I hadn't heard from my job prospects."

Training had been a critical strategy for Walter. "During training I was in class for 32 hours a week, so it was a bit like going to work. At the end of the day, I would discuss the things I had learned with my wife, and we would share how our day went." Two of the certification classes Walter had enrolled in had been paid by the state dislocated worker training fund. When he had thought about the Afghanistan contract, he had negotiated with the school to pay a reduced rate to obtain a third certification that was called Security Plus, or Internet security training. "The best thing I did, and I'm glad that I did it, was to obtain those professional certifications," Walter said. "When I had gone for the interview with the local manufacturing company, the certifications showed them that I was motivated, I had some intelligence, I could learn, and I would persevere."

Walter had kept himself busy and engaged in meaningful activities while unemployed. In reflection, some of these activities remained at the top of his list when asked about what helped him get through each day, each week, each month. "I had developed a walk in my neighborhood," Walter said. "It is probably two miles, either uphill or downhill. So, every morning, before I would leave for training, my wife and I would walk. Over all these years, we have continued to do that walk almost daily."

Reading was another strategy Walter credited with helping him get through unemployment. "I read something like 40 books during those 53 weeks of unemployment. I also had six magazine subscriptions, and I read the *Boston Globe* every day," Walter said. "Reading had a calming influence on me. It had been good for my mental health. Relaxing for my body and engaging for my mind."

There had been the Irish singing too. "Every Friday night, all throughout the period of unemployment, we would go to a local pub where I would join my musician friends and sing Irish songs," Walter said. "It got me out and helped me stay engaged with people. One of the musicians, a guitar player, started dating this woman, and she turned out to be the HR person that provided me the lead to the job at the manufacturing company."

All these years later, Walter credits his military service for preparing him for dealing with life's transitions, such as unemployment. "In the military, there were times that had been very stressful. I had been on the *Tamaroa*, a ship that was 205 feet long. We were on a search and rescue mission, going through 45-foot seas with the risk of capsizing. I said to my boss, Gates, 'Are we going to make it?' And he said, 'I don't know.' These experiences helped put unemployment in context for me."

In reflection, Walter's family provided critical reinforcement. "My wife was my biggest source of support," Walter said. "We have been able to mutually buttress each other, emotionally and financially. That eased the stress for both of us." Walter had a large family – a sister in Pennsylvania, a brother in Australia, two brothers in Virginia, and his mother in Virginia. "My family gets along as well as a family of porcupines," Walter said. "Even so, I could call them up any time. My two brothers had also experienced bouts of unemployment. So, they immediately understood what I was going through. Also, keeping in contact with my military buddies helped too."

Walter had been raised Catholic. He had stopped practicing and attending services years ago. However, during his unemployment stint he had found peace in nature and the woods. "Hunting and getting out in the woods helped me too," Walter said. "I rarely shoot anything. The wonders of nature, just being in the woods while a flock of blackbirds migrate past you or watching a fisher cat jump on a stone wall three feet away from where I had been sitting. These were great days. I often would pause and thank God for the day."

Now that Walter had retired, he had let go of some of the intensity around his structured schedule. "My time structure is now piss poor," Walter said. "I have one constituent, my wife, and no boss. I must wear a watch, not only to tell what time it is, but what day it is too." But retirement was serving Walter well. "I used to joke with my father, when you're retired, every day is Saturday. That is the way it is, and it has been great so far."

Homeless & Resettled
Lou

Lou took our Zoom call from a multipurpose room that appeared to serve as a bedroom and private office space. Lou looked well in his white-collared, bright red Ralph Lauren polo. He appeared more heavy-set than he had back when we had talked previously. He wore the same wire-rim glasses, which sat just below his thick, black eyebrows. Lou explained that there might be some interruptions during our conversation. "Just as an advisory, you may hear me refer to a young lady named Carina. She is my granddaughter," Lou said. "My youngest son and his daughter spend some time with us each week. She is an active two-year-old, and you might see a peek of her on video over the next hour."

Lou and his wife, Fran, have been married for 36 years. Lou held a bachelor's degree in information technology. He previously worked for several large insurance companies in Connecticut and New Hampshire, where he provided computer and information technology support. When I asked how he was doing, Lou said, "Well, it's been a journey."

Since the fall of 2011, Lou, and Fran, lived with and cared for Fran's mother. "The house was large, and with the passing of my father-in-law, it made sense for us to move in," Lou said. "We reduced our cost-of-living and provided help to Fran's aging mother." The house was in Portsmouth, near the school where Fran worked as an administrative assistant. "At the end of 2014, my mother-in-law started to decline in health, and she elected to sell the house in Portsmouth in order to move into a continuing care facility," Lou said.

Lou struggled to find work over the years. His longest span of unemployment extended from 2008 to 2015. "My sister-in-law was the power-of-attorney for financial and healthcare matters involving my mother-in-law," Lou said. "In January of 2015, my sister-in-law informed us that the house was sold and that we needed to find another place to live." Tough financial times hung over Lou like a persistent rain cloud. Lou had not held a full-time job for over seven years. They spent down their savings, and they were just barely getting by on Fran's meager salary. Their credit score tanked over the years as they struggled to pay their bills. They did not have the savings for a security deposit or the first and last month's rent that was typically required. "Fran and I scrambled as best we could. We could not find anywhere to live that we could afford," Lou said. "We could not find anything."

Discouraged by the search for housing, Fran and Lou met with the counselors at Cross Roads House. Cross Roads House provides emergency and transitional shelter to homeless men, women, and children in the New Hampshire seacoast area. Their mission is to meet the immediate needs of the homeless and to provide them with the tools and guidance they need to return to permanent housing.

"The staff at Cross Roads House were skeptical of us," Lou said. "I hate to use stereotypes, but we were well-dressed, and outwardly appeared to be managing, and we owned our vehicles. They were surprised to learn about our situation. It was unusual for couples like us to arrive on their doorstep."

"I explained that we just ran into some bad luck, and that we were trying to get a roof back over our heads," Lou said. "They pressured us a little bit, somewhat in disbelief of our situation. Eventually, they saw that we were motivated to get back on our feet and needed housing to do so."

In late January 2015, Fran and Lou moved into Cross Roads House. "We could not see each other except for meals. In the evenings, after dinner, we would meet in the common area and talk," Lou said. "We could not sleep in the same room. Men were on one side of the shelter and women on the other side of the shelter. When apart, we used text and our phones to communicate. The loss of companionship was tough."

Fran left the shelter to go to work at the school on weekdays. Lou attended workshops on how to rebuild their credit score and finances. He also worked with an employment counselor and searched for work. "I kept applying for jobs, and following the recommendations of the staff at Cross Roads," Lou said. Fran and Lou were grateful for the time they had together. "Fran and I were fortunate to be able to leave from time-to-time," Lou said. "Owning the vehicles made a difference. We had set aside a little of Fran's income for gas for the car. Each weekend we took a drive to Kittery or just into Portsmouth so that we could be outside and walk around a bit. We got out of the shelter, and we could be together for a bit of time."

Fran was on her way back to the shelter after a long day of work at the school. The late May sun had been just setting as she stopped her vehicle at a stop sign. The car in front of her backed up for a pedestrian to access the crosswalk. The driver never looked behind her, and she backed right into Fran's car. "Fortunately, Fran was OK. She experienced a little bit of whiplash," Lou said. "The car was damaged quite a bit. Our insurance covered the damage. We decided to take the settlement for the value of the car rather than fix it. We figured we could get by on one car."

After the automobile accident, things started to look up for Fran and Lou. "I finally landed a job at the National Visa Office located at Pease Air Force Base in June," Lou said. "I was responsible for handling incoming telephone inquiries." The staff at Cross Roads House worked with Fran and Lou on a transition plan, in hopes that they would find housing, especially given Lou's recent employment. "We took the settlement from the car and paid off a few bills. We set aside most of the money for a security deposit for an apartment. We also saved money from Fran's salary to cover the first and last month's rent too."

There was an apartment available in a complex Fran and Lou lived in many years ago when they first moved to Portsmouth. "We applied to the apartment complex and provided our credit history," Lou said. "We knew the property manager. Her kids had grown up with ours, and they previously lived across the street from us." Word arrived in early August that their application was approved. "So, with the help of Cross Roads, we were able to get a U-Haul and retrieve our belongings from storage. By September 1, 2015, we resettled in our own home. It was so nice to have a roof over our heads again, and to be together."

By July 2016, Fran left the school to take a better paying position at Walmart. At about the same time, Lou was laid off from the National Visa office. "Fran suggested that I apply to Walmart," Lou said. "I applied and I was hired almost immediately to work in the produce department." Lou and Fran owned one automobile, so working at the same location was very helpful. "I was able to transfer into the maintenance department eventually," Lou said. "I did store maintenance for Walmart for about three years." After a few years, Fran lost her enthusiasm for her work at Walmart, and she started to search for a different line of work. "Fran was hired by the National Passport Center located on Pease Air Force base at the end of December 2019," Lou said. "Her first day of work was January 2, 2020."

The new position for Fran was a step up in pay and she was on a regular day shift, but the change brought consequences. "I was working a swing shift at Walmart," Lou said. "I would go in at noon and finish my day around 8 p.m. I walked to the bus stop, and used public transportation to get to work, and then Fran would pick me up at night. It was not ideal, but we made it work."

As February approached, the routine of walking a mile to the bus stop, on icy and frozen sidewalks in the dead of winter, became a challenge for Lou. "I decided to apply to the National Passport Center," Lou said. "There was a lot of paperwork, fingerprints, and a financial records check. Gradually, the background stuff came back. The biggest one that was approved was the financial statement. I looked at the report and the bottom of the financial report was stamped 'approved.' I said to myself, 'Yes, this is going to be OK.' The financial statement was the biggest hurdle for me."

Lou was hired full-time as a Passport Support Associate in March 2020, just as the COVID-19 pandemic hit in New Hampshire. He was responsible for processing passport applications, checking the accuracy, ensuring that the photographs were sized properly, and batching them for processing. "I enjoyed the work," Lou said. "I mean it's not anything I expected to be doing, as an IT guy. However, the position does allow me to use my computer skills. I have been able to help people with minor computer problems and with some of the programs." Lou was excelling in his new position too. "There are goals and standards that must be met," Lou said. "I have been able to meet those goals early in the position. They want the work done and they want it done accurately. That is what counts."

Lou and Fran work different shifts. "Some days I take Fran to work at 6:00 a.m.," Lou said. "On those days, I pick her back up at 2:30 p.m. so that I have the vehicle during the day. On other days she takes the car in the morning, and we trade the single vehicle when I leave for my shift which starts at 3:30 p.m."

Lou expressed some nervousness about the impacts of the COVID-19 pandemic on travel and the demand for passports. "These are strange times," Lou said. "We have been so lucky to be working and to have jobs. Things have finally started to improve for us. It's good to be back in a steady routine, and we have been able to start saving money again. We hope things will continue. Given the rough patch we had been through, we are always looking over our shoulders."

Picking Up the Pieces

Social support helped Lou manage through such difficult and challenging times. "Fran and I leaned on each other," Lou said. "She just kept working, and I just kept applying for jobs. We were kind of cheering each other on, reassuring each other. That was the main thing that got us through along with help from others."

In addition to their determination and persistence, Lou and Fran benefited from emotional and financial support, as well as encouragement from others. "My sister-in-law and mother-in-law were extremely supportive of us," Lou said. "For many years, they provided a roof over our heads. Our sons have been helpful too, although we wanted them to be able to make their way in life without us being a burden on them. They both have young families too."

Cross Roads House was a blessing in disguise. "The people at Cross Roads House advocated for us," Lou said. "They cheered us on, and they provided us with solid guidance and direction to get back on our feet. They featured our story on their website as one of their success stories."

Staying active socially and getting out for walks served us well. "Throughout all of this, we kept up with some of our social activities," Lou said. "Fran was a member of the Order of Eastern Star, and I was a Mason. We kept up with our monthly meetings. The socialization helped to normalize the predicament we found ourselves in. Just getting out and walking around on occasion really made a difference."

Lou paused for a moment in reflection, "I feel blessed in so many ways. You learn to appreciate the little things," Lou said. "Being together, having friends, and spending time with our children and grandchildren. We are marching forward, and hopefully we will never have to experience a rough patch like we had been through again."

Staying the Course
Pablo

Pablo was taking his lunch break at the television station when we talked over Zoom. The camera view was dark. "Let me adjust the lighting," Pablo said. "I am in one of the editing suites, and I keep the light dim while I work." Pablo came into focus, and I was able to see the inner workings of the editing suite. I spent a lot of time in and out of editing suites during my tenure at New Hampshire PBS. Often, I was called upon to review rough cuts of stories or to be a second set of eyes and ears on an important piece. I recalled the first time I walked into an editing suite. It was a bit intimidating with all the equipment and a skilled team of editors asking you to quickly provide a critique of a 60-second piece or a 10-second clip.

Clearly and matter-of-factly, Pablo said, "One of the most important elements to the editing suite is the light control. It is paramount to ensure that you have optimal viewing conditions for making critical color decisions." Pablo was seated at a large editing table, and I could see the edges of multiple computer monitors on the work surface. His New Hampshire Public Radio coffee mug was visible along with the mouse to his computer. On the wall directly behind Pablo was a 42-inch plasma screen, used for large screen viewing. On the sidewall, several large documents hung, which looked to display important projects, mapped out with durations and deadlines.

Since our meeting several years ago, Pablo remained unchanged. His midnight-black hair was cut short with a businessmen's professional look, styled with a side part. "Last time we spoke, you were in the process of getting your Ph.D., right?" The question brought back my memory of Pablo's investigative nature, which is one trait of a skilled video or film editor. I replied in the affirmative and talked a bit about my professional work at AARP.

Pablo had worked as a technician at a television station for 26 years before being laid off in 2010. When I spoke with him in the fall of 2011, he had not worked full-time for 19 months. "If you recall, I found part-time work at a television station a couple of months after I had been laid off from my full-time job," Pablo said. "I took a part-time job for a Boston,

Massachusetts, station doing film editing."

During Pablo's job search in 2011, he decided to apply for federal job training funds through the New Hampshire unemployment office. "I wanted to learn computer editing, and that was not something that the training funds typically paid for," Pablo said. "I found a school in Boston, provided the information to the unemployment office, and, despite obstacles, they eventually approved it. I attended seven days of training in Cambridge, Massachusetts, and I learned how to use computer editing software." At the very same time, the television station Pablo was working at made the transition from editing on videotape to computer editing. "The training was helpful," Pablo said. "It was a $3,500.00 investment by the New Hampshire Department of Unemployment Security. I can't discount the importance of the training to my success.

"When I first started working at the television station, I can't recall if I kept on looking externally for full-time work," Pablo said. "I liked working there. They treated their employees well. I liked the management and my co-workers." There were pros and cons to Pablo's part-time job. "The only bad part about working part-time was that I was not eligible for benefits," Pablo said. "I was hoping to become full-time at the television station, but job openings occur relatively infrequently. Some of the positions are outside of my area of expertise. Others went to people who had longer tenure at the television station than me."

Pablo enjoyed the flexibility of working part-time. "I worked an average of three days a week, though it varied, and some weeks I might have worked five days," Pablo said. "The money was good, and I enjoyed the time off. It was a pretty good gig. I edited news footage. The television station does a lot of news, so there was always work." The television station was state-of-the-art. "They were always updating the equipment," Pablo said. "They taught you how to use the new equipment, and when they wanted you to do something different, they would train you. They kept me regularly employed on a part-time basis and invested in my skill development, so I did not see any reason to leave. Nine years later and I am still working in the same part-time job."

Picking Up the Pieces

After all these years, Pablo steadfastly credits his part-time job and engaging in meaningful activities as helping him to manage unemployment. "The part-time job has provided me with a sense of satisfaction and purpose," Pablo said. "It is what kept me going. If I hadn't found the part-time job, I would have gotten discouraged. Even though it's always been my goal to be employed full-time again, just having the part-time job to go to, and to know my work is appreciated, helped me cope with what would otherwise be a very depressing situation."

Part-time work fulfilled the manifest function of employment for Pablo. "For a part-time job, the pay is good," Pablo said. "I've always been frugal and good at managing my money. I've never gone into debt." Pablo also found satisfaction in doing things for himself. "I do auto repair work," Pablo said. "Just yesterday, my directional signal wasn't working. I pulled the whole thing apart. It was corroded. I cleaned it up, put it back together, and now it works. So I saved the $50 to $100 I would have paid to a repair shop. I also find these kinds of things rewarding."

Pablo's part-time job also provided for the latent functions of work. "It wasn't just the money," Pablo said. "The part-time job provided me with a sense of purpose, social interaction, and everything else that comes with employment, like a schedule and contributing to something bigger than yourself." Pablo offered this advice: "If someone is laid off and they can find a part-time job, even if it is not in their field of expertise, it will still offer tremendous benefit and help to stabilize a very unsteady situation."

Pablo credited social interactions at work and home with buffering the impacts of unemployment. "Social interaction is important," Pablo said. "When you lose a job, you automatically lose all the interaction that you had with your coworkers. You must replace it with something. You must find a way to stay connected with people."

Pablo leaned into friends and family. "I have some friends here at the condominium complex where I live," Pablo said. "There are a couple of guys my age in the building. We would get together each week and just talk. It was helpful to me, especially since I lived alone." Pablo's parents lived in the adjacent town. "I made it a point to visit my parents each week." In addition, Pablo tried to stay connected to his sibling. "Funny thing is that I was never close to my brother growing up. Now, whenever I call him, he will keep me on the phone for well over an hour. It is just so different from the way it used to be."

Investing time in special interests and hobbies was another key strategy for Pablo. "When we spoke in 2011, I told you how interested I was in current events, news, and politics," Pablo said. "I still listen to all forms of news and talk radio. I am a political junkie. Staying up-to-date with what was going on kind of pulled me through on those tough days." Pablo also discovered he had a talent for pitching and selling everyday items. "I owned a bunch of items that were around the house that I no longer needed or wanted," Pablo said. "I didn't want to just throw them out, so I decided to sell them on Craigslist. I took some pictures, wrote some ads, and posted everything. Soon, I was getting calls on all the items I posted and selling the stuff. Every time I sold something, I got this little rush of adrenaline and feeling of satisfaction and accomplishment."

Pablo started to think about turning his hobby into a business venture. "It is funny, just today I sold the old electric typewriter that I had in college," Pablo said. "It was purchased for $50. The women who bought it was so grateful. I have been thinking that I could do more of this when I retire and create a little extra money for myself."

Pablo was a music aficionado. "The other thing that helped me cope with unemployment was music," Pablo said. "I am a music lover. I buy and listen to all types of music. I research the artist, learn the backstory of their careers. I investigate the story behind the song, who wrote it, what inspired it, the musicians that contributed to it, and when it was recorded. It gave me something meaningful to do with my time, provided intellectual stimulation, and it was rewarding, and still is."

When I spoke with Pablo in 2011, the thought of retirement had crossed his mind. "I had been preparing for retirement with a 401(K) and IRA," Pablo said. "I started saving for retirement when I was 22 years old. No matter what, I invested $2000.00 each year into my IRA. I thought to myself, 'If I can't find full-time work again, I would retire early and get off the treadmill.'"

In 2020, Pablo offered a different perspective. "I think I would be crazy to leave the position now," Pablo said. "I lucked out by ending up at the television station. I am 61 years old, and I am happy to put my time in and retire when I turn age 65 or so. If I had the opportunity to step into a full-time position, I would accept the position. Otherwise, I am quite content working part-time."

Deferred Retirement
Tzippora

A while ago, when I spoke to Tzippora, she had been recovering from breast cancer treatment and was on the verge of losing her home. Now another loss hung in the air. "It is nice to hear from you again," Tzippora responded in an e-mail. "I am so very sorry it took me so long to reply. My 99-year-old mother just recently passed away, and I have been consumed with closing out her estate."

I finally connected with Tzippora one late October afternoon in 2020 on Zoom. It quickly became clear that she was proficient with Zoom. She was in her home office, her back faced a blank wall, which prevented background distractions. The picture was clear, and the camera was set with a concise headshot. Her eyes were the same dark chestnut I remembered, and her hair remained jet black, curly, and worn at shoulder length.

At the start of our call, I expressed my sympathies for the loss of her mother. "My daughter and I were very close to my mother," Tzippora said. "With my mom, it was always us three girls. We traveled together, and we did all kinds of activities together, right up to the very end. I am so grateful for the strong bond we had."

I asked about her journey back to employment. "It hasn't exactly been easy. It took me until January 2012, to find another position." Tzippora was a technical writer, and she had over 30 years of experience. "I worked with a hiring agency and the woman assigned to me was unbelievable. She referred me to three or four different contracts, so I was able to work full-time on a steady basis since early 2012."

Tzippora had put in long days. "The last three or four contracts were with companies in Boston," Tzippora said. "I never knew what the traffic was going to be like between Portsmouth and Boston on a given day. Many nights, I arrived back in Portsmouth late and I fell prey to fast food for dinner instead of cooking something healthy at home."

In March 2020, everything changed. "When the COVID-19 pandemic hit, the company shifted to teleworking, and I was able to work from home. My Mahjong friend said to me one day in late spring, 'Boy, Linda, you are looking great.' That is when I realized what a toll the commute had on me. I never felt right. I was always tired. I looked tired and acted tired."

Tzippora had worked for big financial companies. "Unfortunately, I'm on the job hunt again," Tzippora said. "My contract ended in June 2020, and the recruiter I was working with at the agency retired. Now with the pandemic, it's terrible for everyone." Tzippora, once again, was faced with a job search. "Most recently, I was working on internal company documentation, so I did not have the opportunity to update my skills. I can see that I am at a big disadvantage because of that. Companies are now looking for experience with new software tools and methodologies, like information mapping. The other thing is that biotech and medical have exploded for writers, and I have no experience in those areas."

As bleak as things might have been, Tzippora was optimistic. "I saw two openings for technical writers with companies I had worked for before. Both companies had provided positive reviews of my work. I have applied to both positions," Tzippora said. "I am hopeful that one of the companies will contact me. I believe both companies are looking to bring technical writing in-house, which would mean I would have a shot at a regular full-time job, with benefits and a retirement plan."

There was a silver lining to the pandemic. "Both companies have advertised the positions as telework positions," Tzippora said. "Teleworking is very appealing to me. I want to achieve a better balance in my life. I have been eating healthy, and I have lost weight. So, without the commute, I have taken the time to care for myself. I have noticed a big difference in my quality of life."

Finances remained a struggle for Tzippora. "When I applied for my unemployment in July 2020, there was a delay in the payments," Tzippora said. "I never received payment until September. I had to live off my 2019 income tax return until I received a retroactive lump-sum unemployment check. Starting in September, I received a regular unemployment check." There was always a demand on Tzippora's limited resources. "Unfortunately, with the contract work, anytime I was able to set money aside, something would come up. I had to replace my refrigerator a few years ago, then I needed a new stove, and then my daughter's school loans kicked in. The education loans are about $1,000 a month. So, I am watching every penny really closely and cutting as many corners as I can."

Tzippora had visions of retirement. "I am 66 years old, so technically I could retire," Tzippora said. "I can't afford to retire. I have no retirement savings. Every time I was laid off, I needed to dip into my savings to survive. I know that I have Social Security to look forward to, but that is not enough to survive. I am thinking that I will work for maybe another 10 years if I can. After that, I hope to come up with something I can do part-time on the side to supplement my Social Security payments."

Oddly enough, Tzippora, like Pablo, the television news editor, was thinking about starting a small business venture by selling things on Craigslist or eBay. "It has crossed my mind, with all the stuff I have, and all my mother's things in storage, that I could sell these things. I hate to just recycle them or toss them out," Tzippora said. "I am a skilled writer, I am pretty good with a camera and the computer, so I think this might be an option. I could dispose of some unwanted items, make a little money, and possibly promote my services to others."

Picking Up the Pieces

As Tzippora looked back over the years, social support emerged as a key coping strategy for safeguarding her well-being. "At the time, I made a good friend who was in the same boat as me," Tzippora said. "She was a technical writer too. We would go to networking meetings and events together. We were job-search buddies. We stayed close over the years. She recently retired and moved back to Indiana."

In the past, Tzippora had started a networking group. "The group grew to nearly 30 people who attended the networking meetings regularly. Almost everyone eventually found jobs, and we decided to disband the group." Spending time networking remained a worthy cause and an important job search strategy. "Given COVID-19, many of the networking groups have gone online, mostly through Zoom. It is still helpful. I can attend and get help with interview techniques and skill-building tips. The challenge is that we know each other's faces, but we don't really know each other."

I asked Tzippora what practices or activities, in hindsight, helped her through the rough patches. "Oh, my original Mahjong group and my religious community were important to me. When we talked previously, I had just gone through breast cancer and radiation treatments. My mahjong group was my lifeline during that time. I have maintained those close connections through life's ups and downs. They were a good support when my mom was sick. All I had to do was call on them, and they were there for me."

Proactively reaching out to cultivate existing and new relationships was a comfortable and proven practice for Tzippora. "I started another mahjong group before COVID-19 hit," Tzippora said. "I have attended two mahjong groups weekly. These people know a bit more about me, and I have deep connections with them, so I am a lot more comfortable with them online as compared to the networking groups, where people are barely acquaintances."

Tzippora valued family relationships. "Over the years, I have worked hard to maintain connections with my two brothers. One brother is just not a proactive communicator, and the other brother, Alexander, who my mother lived with for years, has always been negative towards me. He will say things like, 'You have an awful life.' I shrug it off because I am perfectly happy with my life."

As difficult as it was, Tzippora continued to reach out to be a part of Alexander's life. "Now that my mother has passed and Alexander's wife and son have moved out, he is living alone in a 2500 square-foot home," Tzippora said. "I make it a point to visit him once a week. The telephone just doesn't work with him." Tzippora remained close to her daughter, too. "My daughter got married last September. She is happy. She married a terrific guy. I am so happy for her. She lives 45 minutes from me, and we still see each other quite a bit. She has always been a big help to me. Connections with family and friends have got me through the rough patches over the years."

In addition to leaning into social connections, Tzippora used her time in meaningful ways to help balance the ups and downs of searching for work. "I spent a fair amount of time cooking when I was laid off in 2011, and now I am doing the same thing," Tzippora said. "I like to be inventive when I cook. I will create something in my head and try it out. My daughter is still a little puzzled about how I do that. I have always found cooking to be a way to use my creativity, and it helps me relax." In addition to cooking, Tzippora collected cookbooks. "I have two bookshelves full of cookbooks," Tzippora said. "Now I will inherit my mother's collection as well."

I asked Tzippora if there was anything else that helped her

cope with unemployment over the years. "I enjoy crafting and making things. It has helped me financially too. I was able to make the gifts I gave to family members and friends. I enjoyed that."

While Tzippora has hit another rough patch, all was not doom. "This summer has not been the greatest, with losing my mother and having to look for work again," Tzippora said. "I have not been sitting around saying, 'Oh poor me,' which I might have done in the past." When I spoke with Tzippora previously, she had just finished monthly personal development courses offered by Landmark Education. "I know there were many years when I was sort of a negative person. I had taken these courses and they really helped me then, and I still rely on what I learned. I was able to make a shift, and I started looking for the good in situations." Today, the practices are still in play. "I have a calendar with a saying a day. First thing in the morning when I get up, I read the quote of the day. They are very positive and help me to focus on gratitude and being authentic."

People noticed the shift in Tzippora then and now. "A lot of times I would be hiding. I was not authentic," Tzippora said. "In my original mahjong group, there would be times when the group would discuss something, and I would disagree. I would not voice my opinion. After going through the Landmark Education courses, I started to speak up more and share my opinion. I started talking more freely. Even now, that has helped me to truly show up as the person that I am with people and groups."

As I started to close out the conversation, Tzippora smiled, took a deep breath, and said, "Life is good for me. I am healthy. I have my family and friends. My daughter is doing well. I am happy with how things are going in my life, even though I plan to delay retirement and I am unemployed now."

11. Don't Sit Idle

Your job or career form a big part of your life and identity. Throughout this book, in their own words, unemployed people shared the lessons they learned about how to take care of their well-being while figuring out what was next in the aftermath of being laid off.

Nested within the individual stories and self-reflection on unemployment, the five strategies to safeguard well-being emerged. Each strategy was cited, in some way, as being helpful to coping with unemployment. Walter, Pablo, and Tzippora spoke about how they used their time in meaningful ways by enhancing their skills, engaging with a hobby, or working part-time. Elena and Lou underscored how they made use of the power of agency and determination. Conserving resources and frugality were a way of life for all.

The importance of people and social relationships appeared as a key factor. Each person described the social support they received as critical to helping them cope with the challenges associated with unemployment. Uniformly, they credited having at least one constant person in their life who steadied them and supported them. For some, that person was a spouse, and for others, it was a family member, a friend, or a work colleague. That special supportive relationship was like a talisman that confers on its bearer protective and stabilizing powers. The social support provided was the one thing that enabled everyone to carry on and tap into the other four strategies to steady the bumpy ride.

You may be reading this and feeling dispirited because you don't believe that you have someone that cares about you and that can serve as your talisman. Your natural reaction might be to continue to withdraw from friends and family and social interaction in general. You need to do just the opposite. Reach out. Social contact is an antidote to stress. The person you talk to doesn't need to offer you the answers; they do need to be a good listener. If you do not have family and friends to tap into, reach out to a free employment counselor or join a job club. It is never too late to renew your social relationships. Seek out new people who are also looking for work by taking a class or attending a job fair. Check out community groups you are interested in, like a walking group or book club or volunteer.

You are not alone on this journey. Within the stories shared in this book, I hope that you found a companion with a shared experience, inspiration to persevere, or a tip for dealing with the impact of job loss. You can seize control of your situation by putting in place the five strategies to piece your well-being back together and support your mental and physical health. There are people who will help you. Be proactive and reach out. Above all else, don't sit idle.

"May you never forget that when it was hard, and you were overwhelmed, and felt afraid, and walked alone, and felt invisible, and didn't have the answers, and couldn't see the way, and wanted to give-up, you kept going."

-Nakeia Homer

Acknowledgements

I would like to acknowledge and thank those who have joined me on the journey to publish this book.

Jackie Heuser, former Director of the NH Office of Workforce Opportunity and Chris Beauvais, former Workforce Investment Act Statewide Administrator, for their tremendous collaboration on my original research. Without their support and cooperation, the research would not have been possible.

Grace Lessner, a colleague and dear friend, for her razor-sharp editorial eye, consistent support, and enduring belief in me and the work.

Richard Adams Carey for his early editorial support, descriptive writing coaching, encouragement, and sensitivity in helping me to build on my earlier work to make it better.

Janice Gregory, a long-time friend, for her review and critique of the entire manuscript, sharing a wealth of information and literary resources, and for our many discussions about the book and her thoughtful suggestions about ways to improve it.

Maile Black at Winter Island Press for her assistance and guidance.

Tom Holbrook of Holbrook Author Services for his wise counsel, editing, formatting, cover design, and end-to-end publishing support. The amazing feat of publishing this book would not have been possible without his stellar and enthusiastic support throughout.

Finally, my husband John for his love and support over the years, and to our bloodhounds Spencer and Sadie, who have crossed the rainbow bridge and to Baxter, our current bloodhound. All have kept me honest over the years with their big snouts letting me know that it was time to step away from writing and the computer.

About the Author

As a nonprofit executive and educator for over three decades, Kelly A. Clark, PhD has worked with many individuals making employment transitions, both voluntary and involuntary. Her research on how people get through job loss and maintain their well-being led her to delve into the experiences of older unemployed individuals who had careers in white-collar and blue-collar occupations. Clark has been an executive at AARP for nearly 20 years, and serves on the NH Workforce Innovation Board. She previously led the NH Workforce Opportunity Council.

Clark's PhD dissertation research, which was published in the *Applied Journal on Quality of Life* and featured in several articles, explored the life experience of long-term unemployed baby boomers who remained upbeat despite lengthy and discouraging job searches and the impact on their personal lives.

Clark has a bachelor's degree in accounting and finance from the University of Maine, Orono; a master's degree in public policy and management from the University of Southern Maine, Edmund S. Muskie School of Public Service; and both a master's degree in human development and PhD in human and organizational systems from Fielding Graduate University.

She lives in New Hampshire with her husband and their bloodhound, Baxter. Connect with Kelly on LinkedIn, and visit her website KellyClarkAuthor.com.

Endnotes

_____

Introduction

[1] AARP (2024). Employment Data Digest. Retrieved on April 9, 2024 from March 2024 Employment Data Digest (aarp.org)

Chapter 3

[1] Perron, Rebecca (2018). *The Value of Experience: AARP Multicultural Work and Jobs Study*. Washington, DC: AARP Research, July 2018. doi.org/10.26419/res.00177.000

Chapter 4

[1] Morning Consult (2020). Retrieved on June 15, 2020 from morningconsult.com/2020/04/02/coronavirus-recession-unemployment-poll/

[2] Pew Research Center (2018). Retrieved on June 20, 2020 from www.pewresearch.org/fact-tank/2018/01/31/more-adults-now-share-their-living-space-driven-in-part-by-parents-living-with-their-adult-children/

[3] Newberry, C. (2012). *The hands-on guide to surviving adult children living at home*. Nuru Guides

[4] Niederhaus, S.G., & Graham, J. (2007). *Together again: A creative guide to successful multigenerational living*. Landham, MD: Evans & Company

[5] Quilty, D. (2022). Retrieved on April 24, 2022 from

www.moneycrashers.com/best-bartering-swapping-websites/

6 Cahn, E.S. (2004). *No More Throw-Away People.* Washington, D.C.: Essential Books Ltd.

Chapter 5

1 Mayo Clinic (2019). Retrieved on June 25, 2020 from www.mayoclinic.org/healthy-lifestyle/fitness/in-depth/exercise/art-20048389

2 Roots, H., (2017). 10 ways reading more makes you an excellent employee. Business Insider UK. Retrieved on December 10, 2020 from www.businessinsider.com/10-benefits-of-reading-that-will-make-you-more-employable-2017-5

3 Corporation for National & Community Service (2013). Volunteering as a pathway to employment: Does volunteering increase odds of finding a job for the out of work? Retrieved from: www.nationalservice.gov/sites/default/files/upload/employment_research_report.pdf

Chapter 6

1 Canadian Mental Health Association (2018). *Social Support* Retrieved from https://cmha.ca/documents/social-support

Chapter 7

1 Deutschendorf, H. (2016). "7 Habits that can help you become more optimistic." *Fast Company*. Retrieved from www.fastcompany.com/3055069/7-habits-that-can-help-you-

become-more-optimistic?cid=search

2 Lama, D. And Tutu, D. (2016). *The Book of Joy*. New York, New York: Penguin Random House

3 Ibid, 99

4 Kos, B. Cognitive Reframing Exercise by AgileLeanLife.com Retrieved from agileleanlife.com/cognitive-reframing

5 Rake (2018). *12 Awesome Mantras for Job-Seekers*. Retrieved on June 2, 2019 from medium.com/@getrake/12-awesome-mantras-for-job-seekers-e16a37580475

6 Thoreau, retrieved from www.walden.org/what-we-do/library/thoreau/thoreau-quotations/

Chapter 8

1 Napper, P. & Rao, A. (2019). *The Power of Agency*. New York, NY: St. Martin's Press

2 Ibid, 16-17

Chapter 9

1 O'Mear, R. (2017). *Pause*. New York, NY: Penguin Random House

Made in the USA
Columbia, SC
26 August 2024